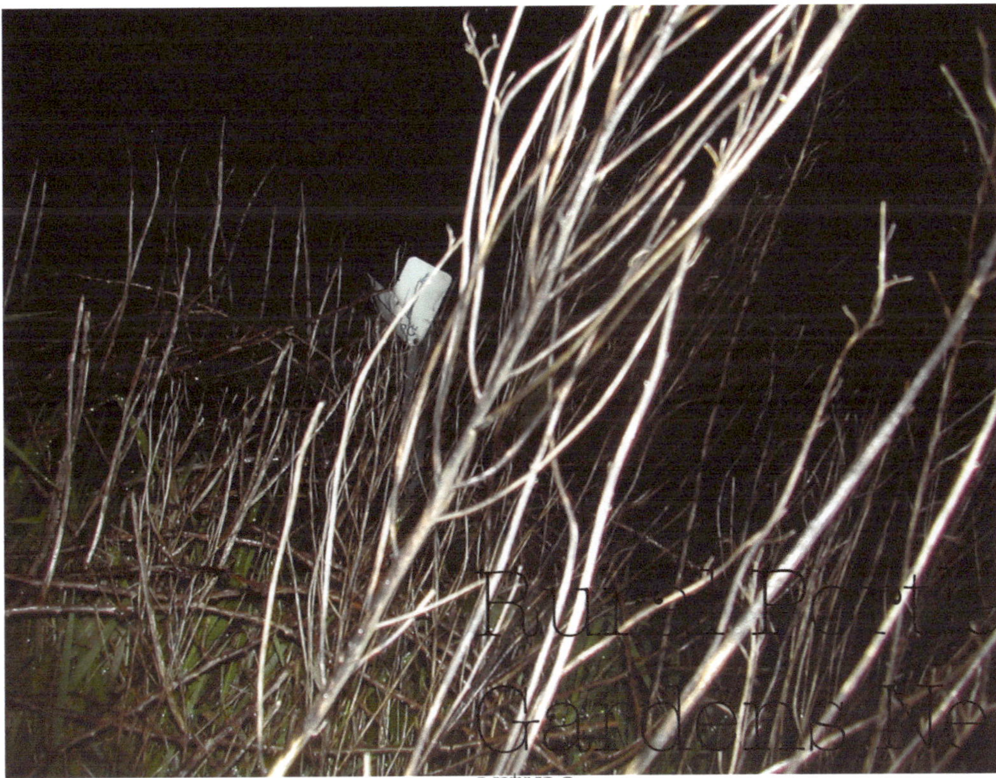

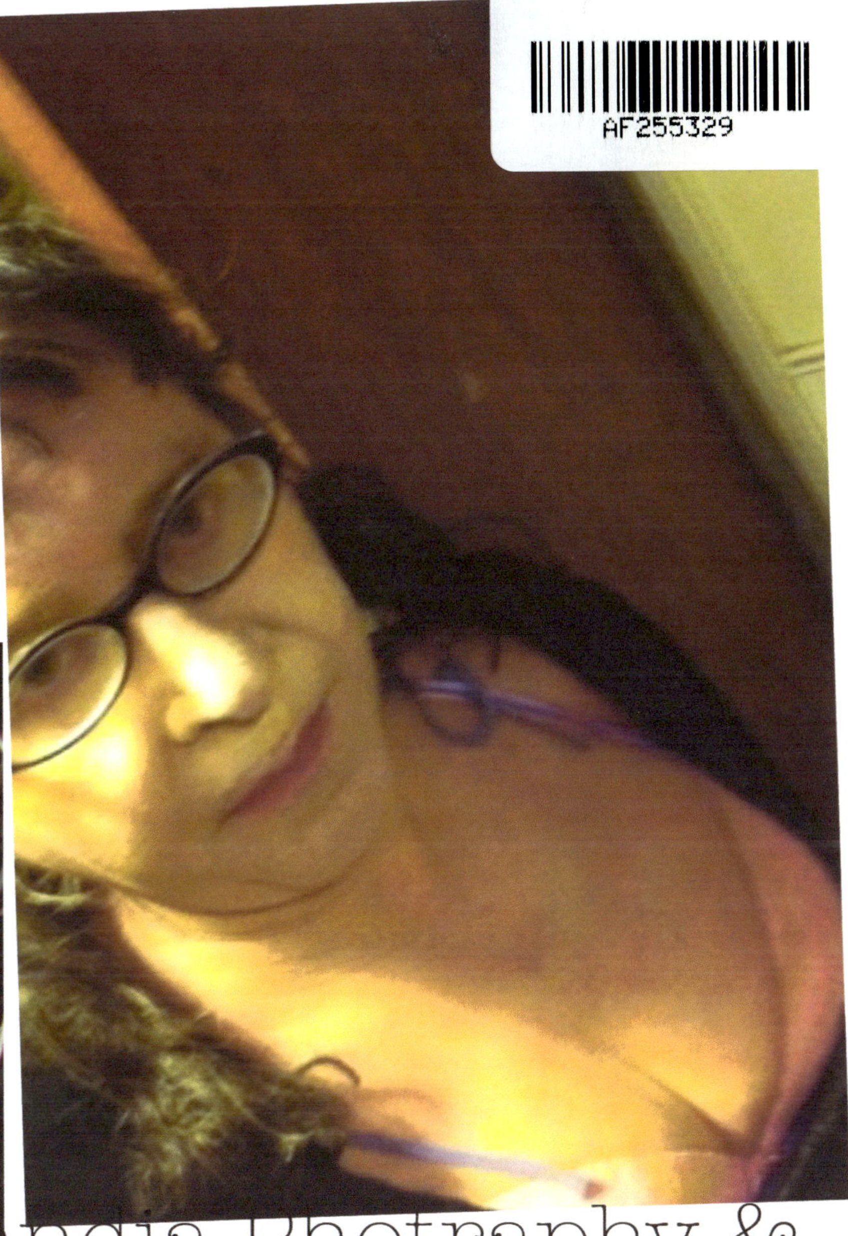

Rui & Portlandia Photraphy & Gardens Near Railgardens
by andrea artina

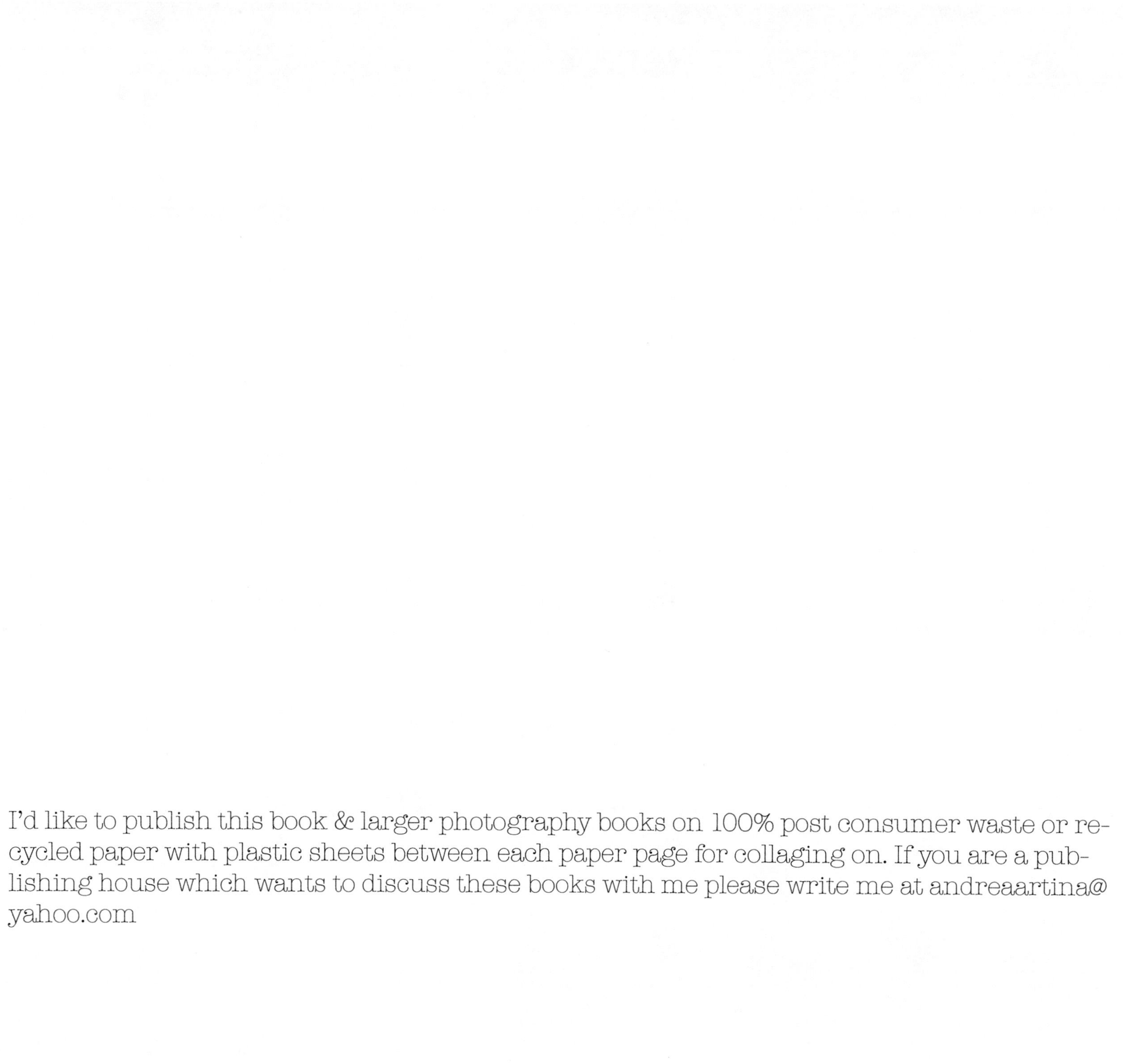

I'd like to publish this book & larger photography books on 100% post consumer waste or recycled paper with plastic sheets between each paper page for collaging on. If you are a publishing house which wants to discuss these books with me please write me at andreaartina@yahoo.com

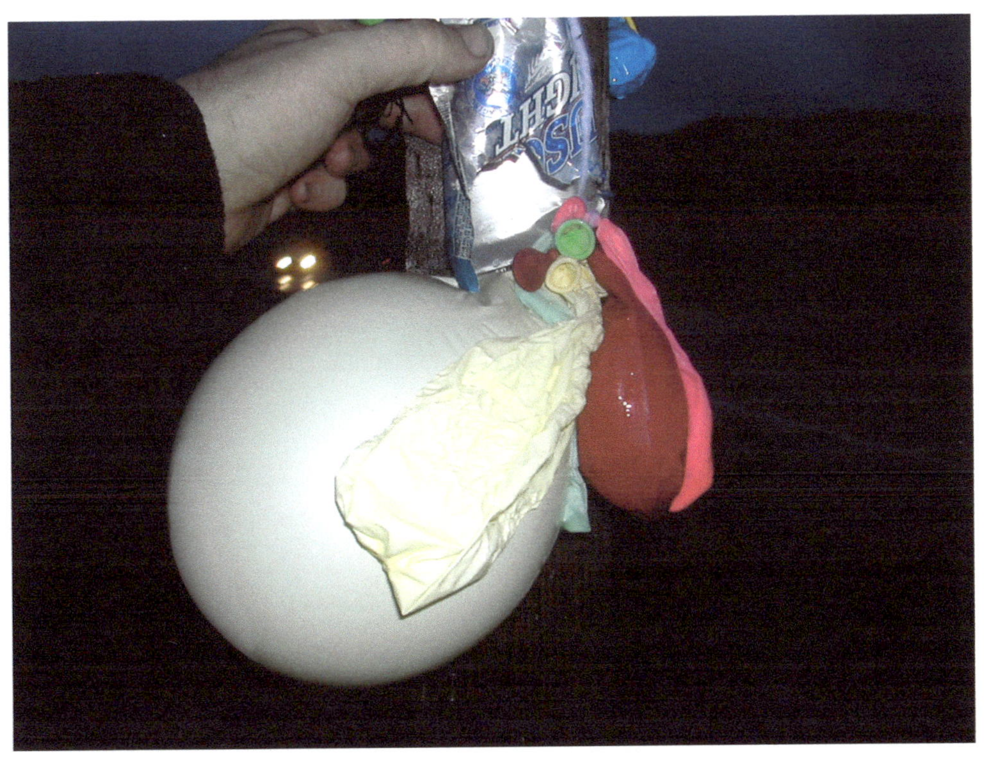

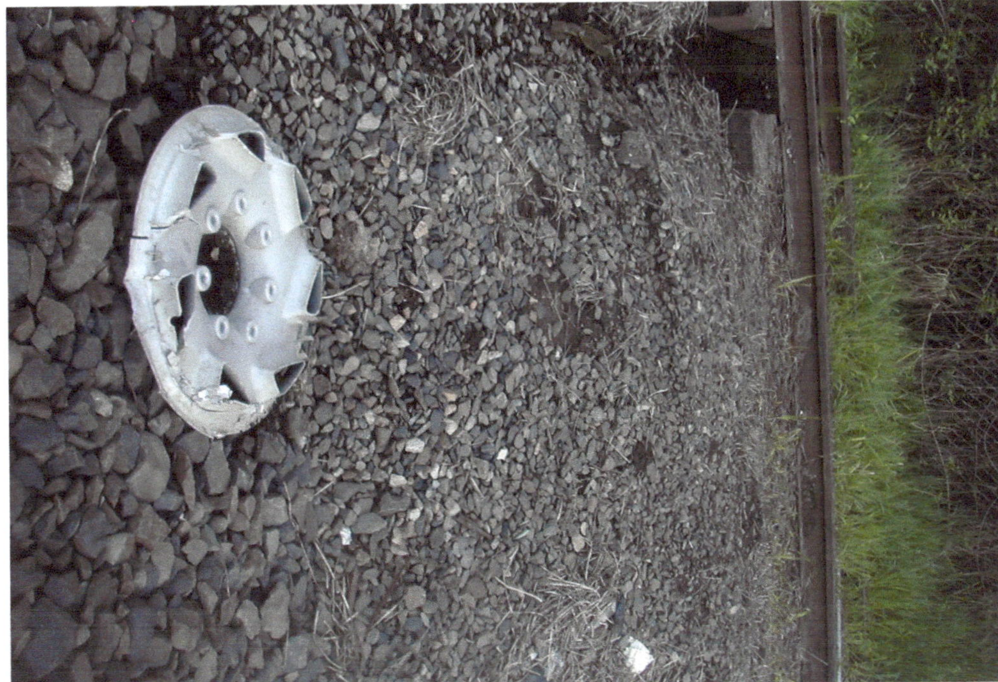

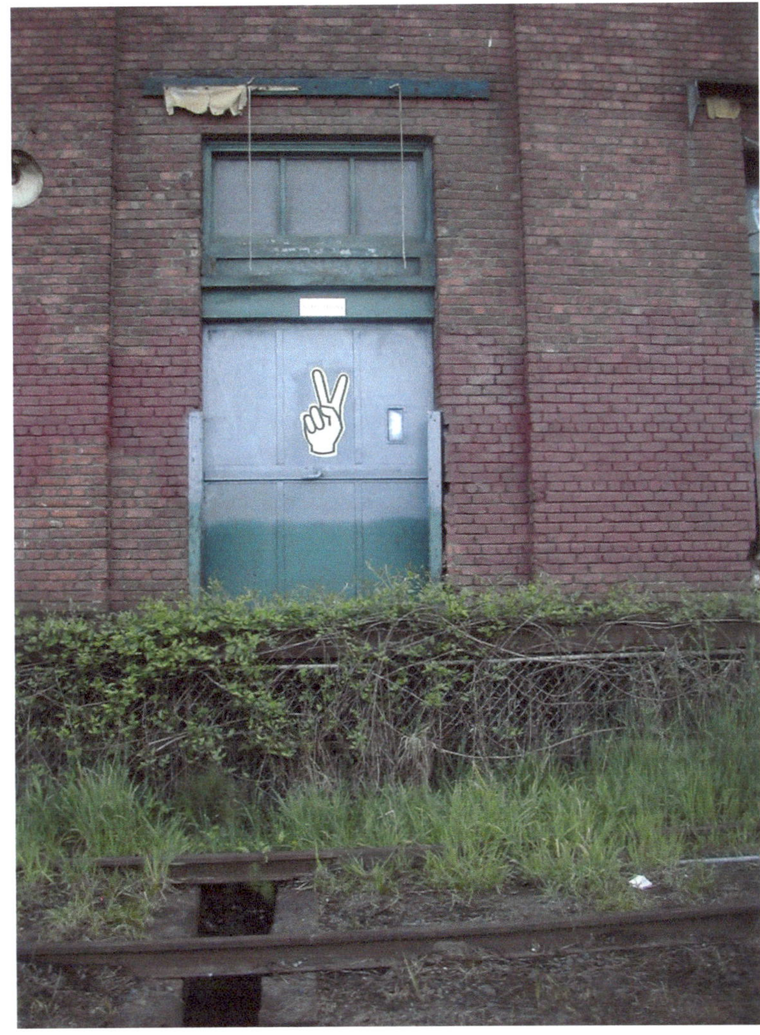

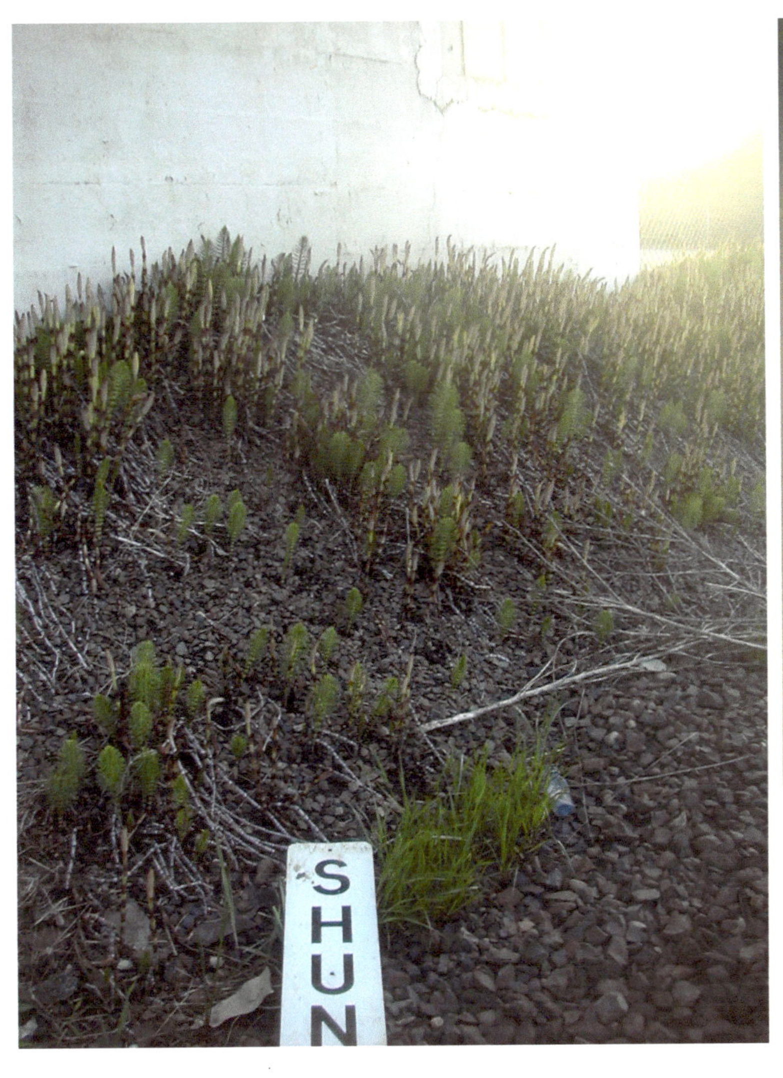

SHUN

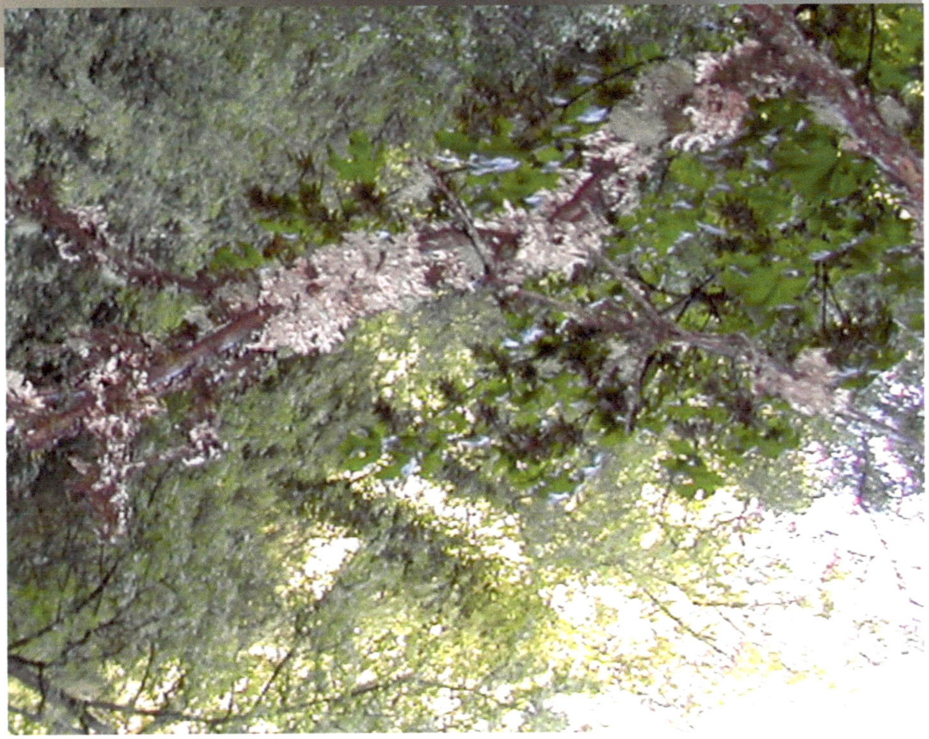

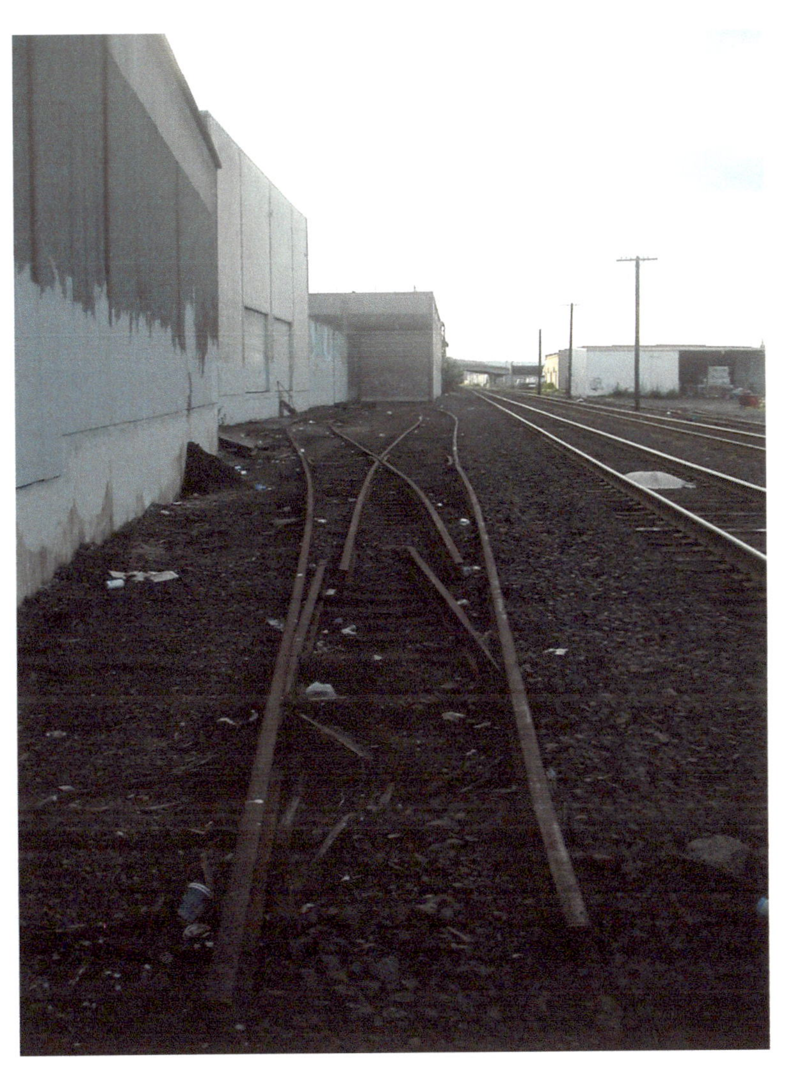

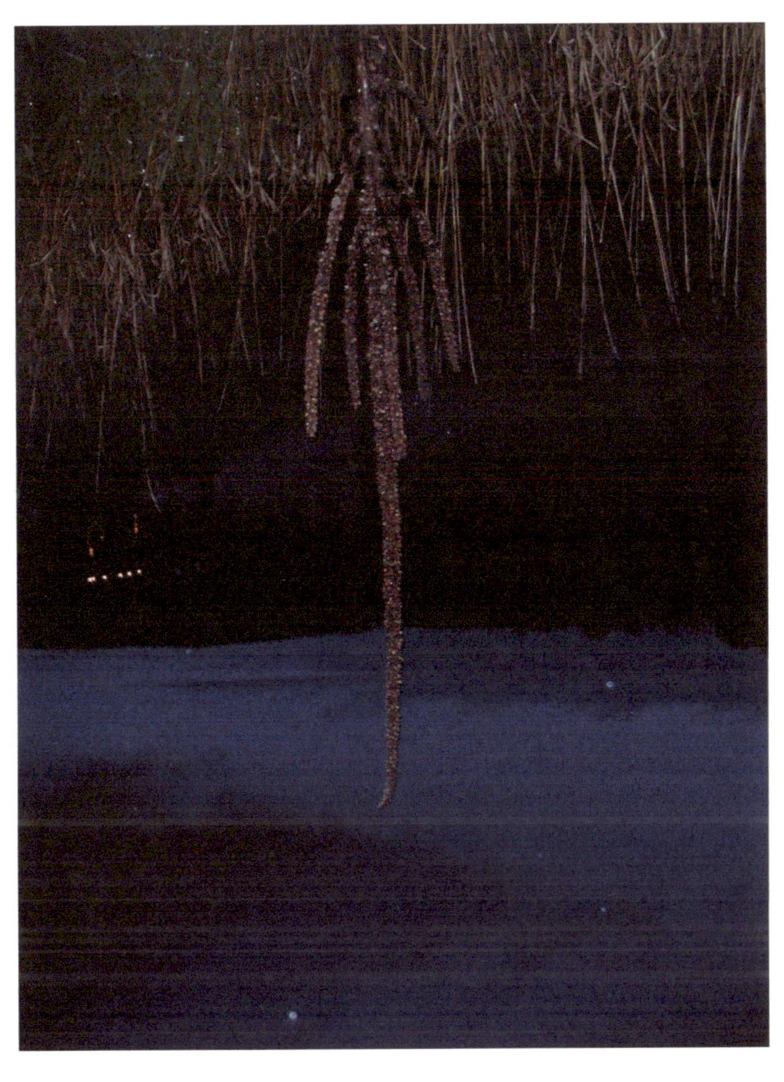

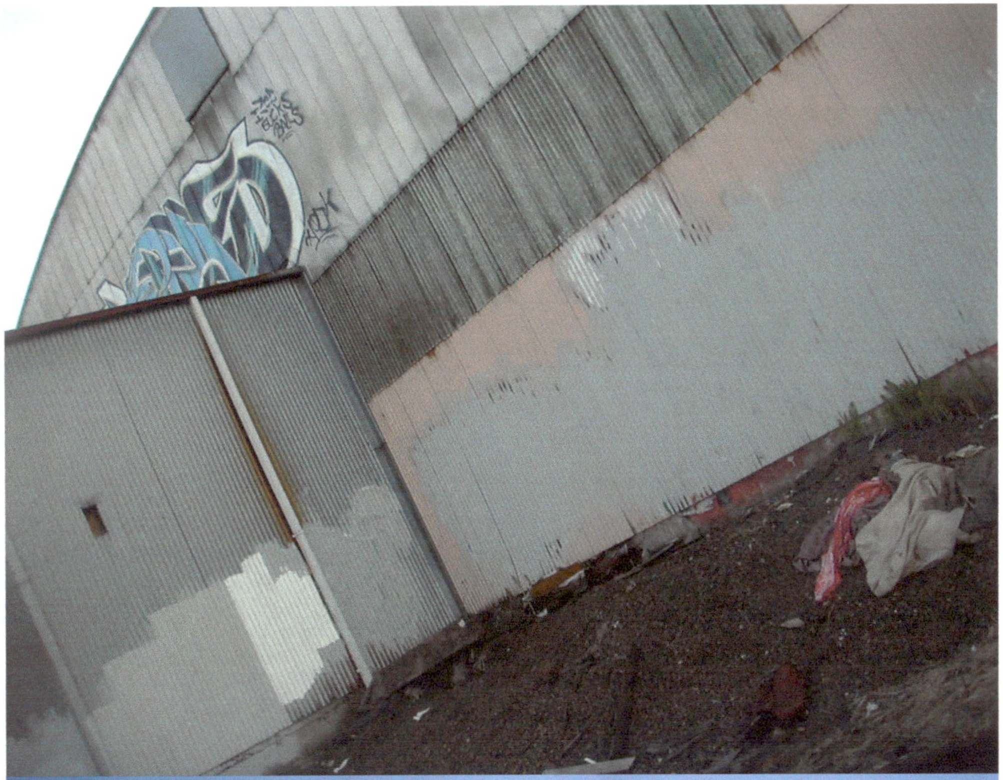

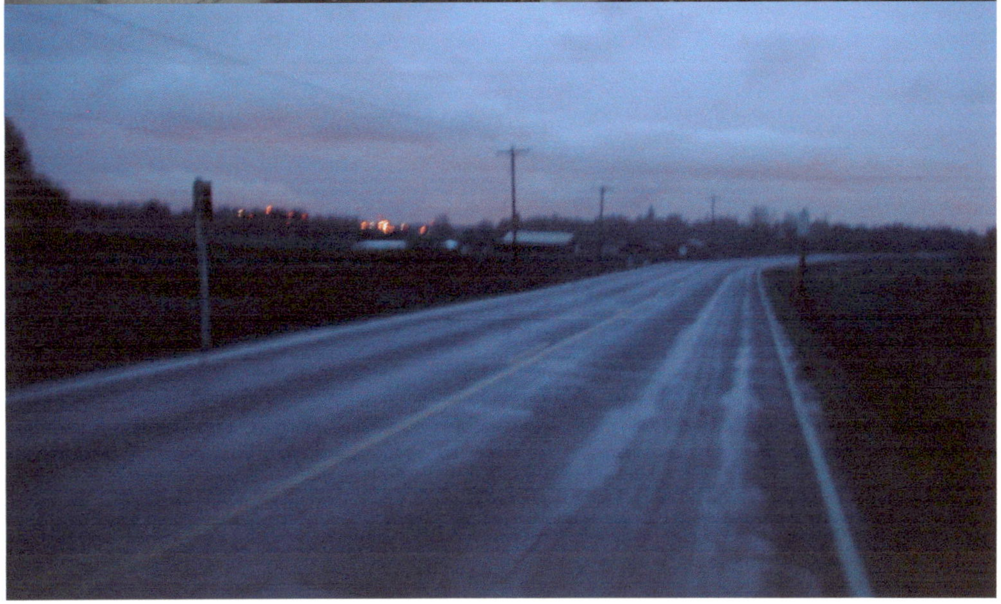

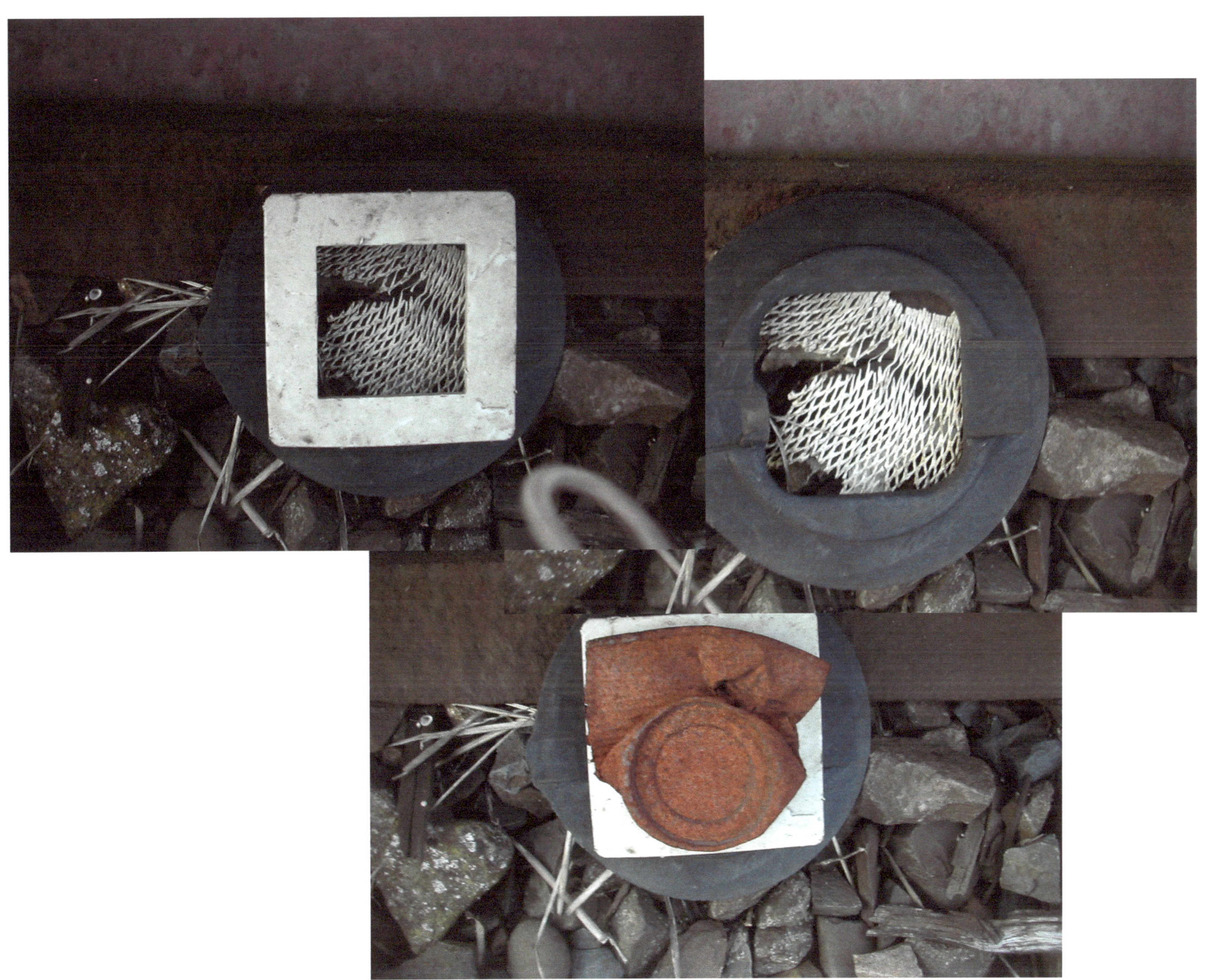

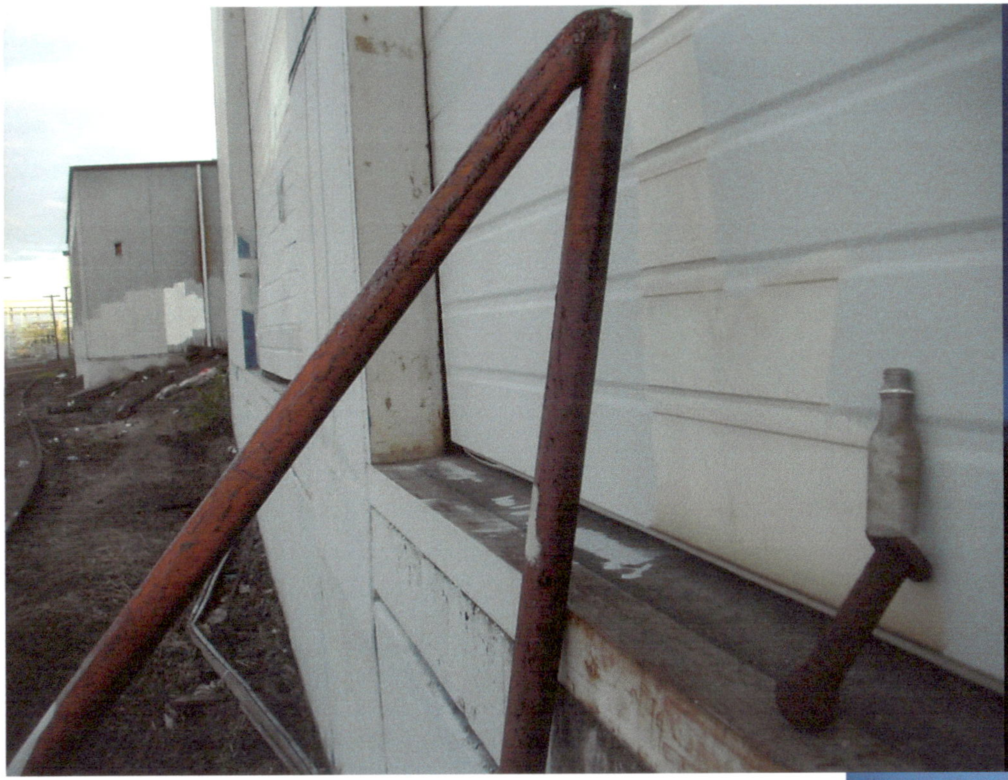

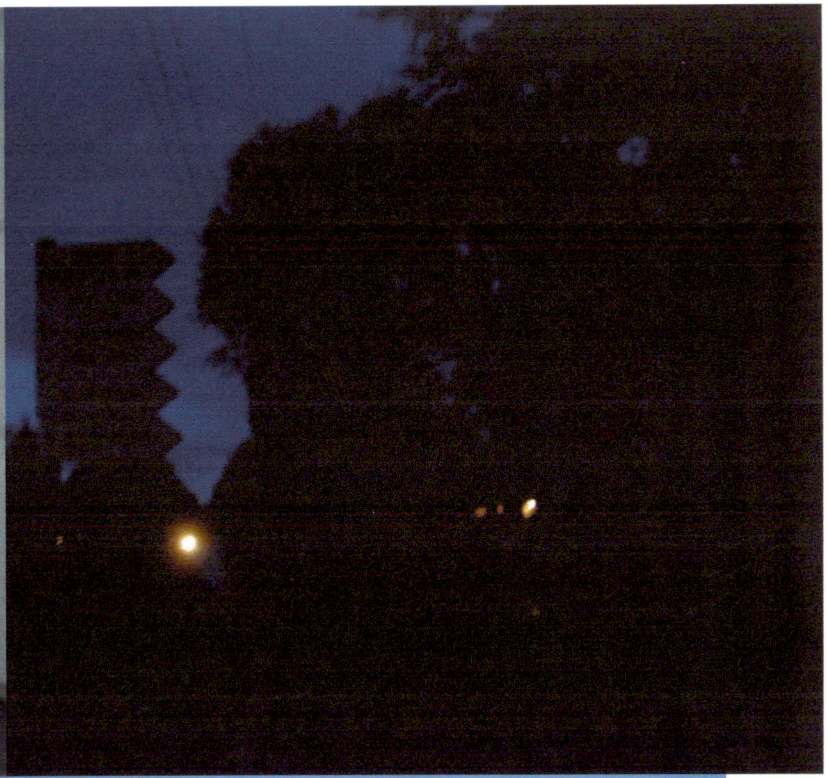

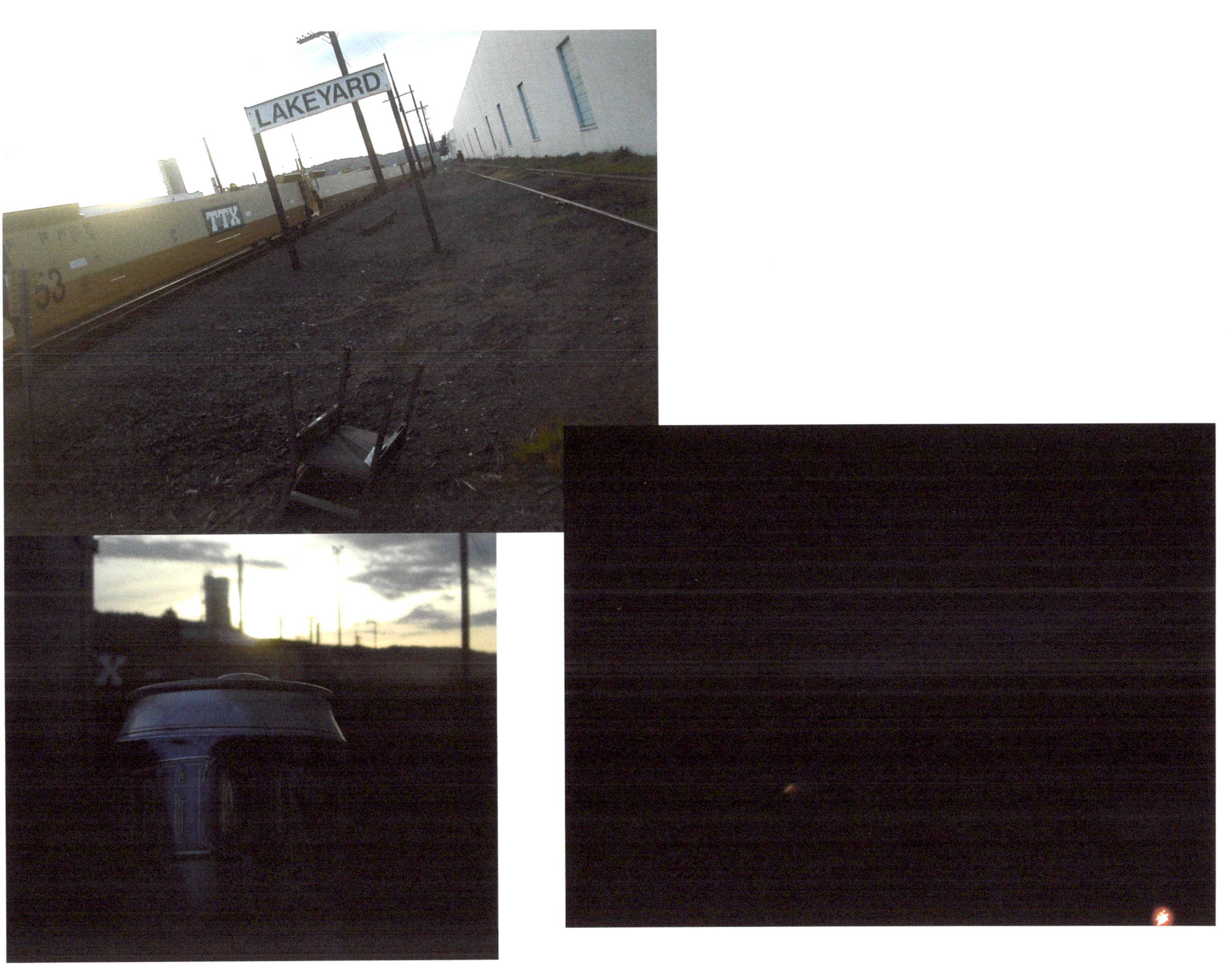
LAKEYARD
TTX
53

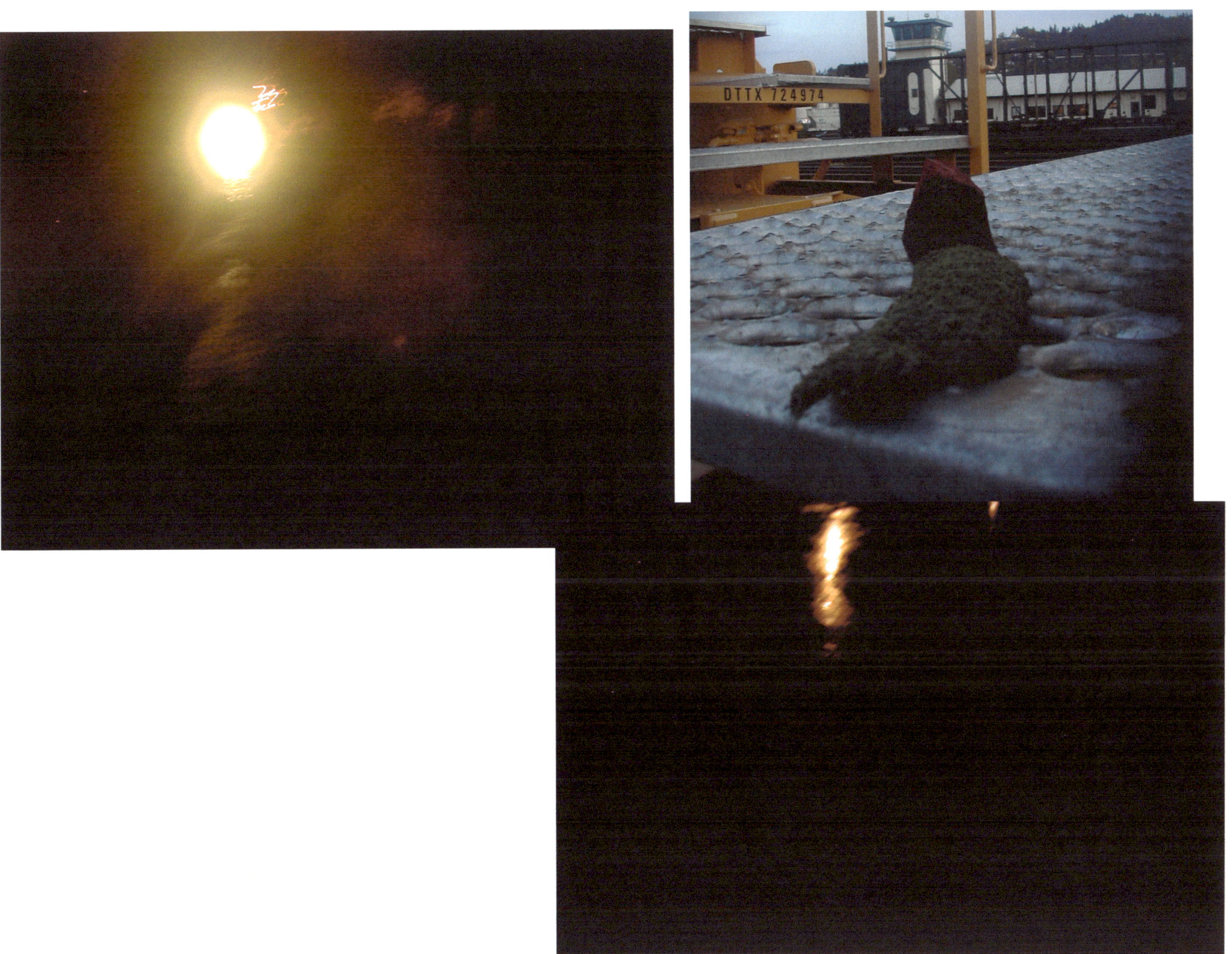

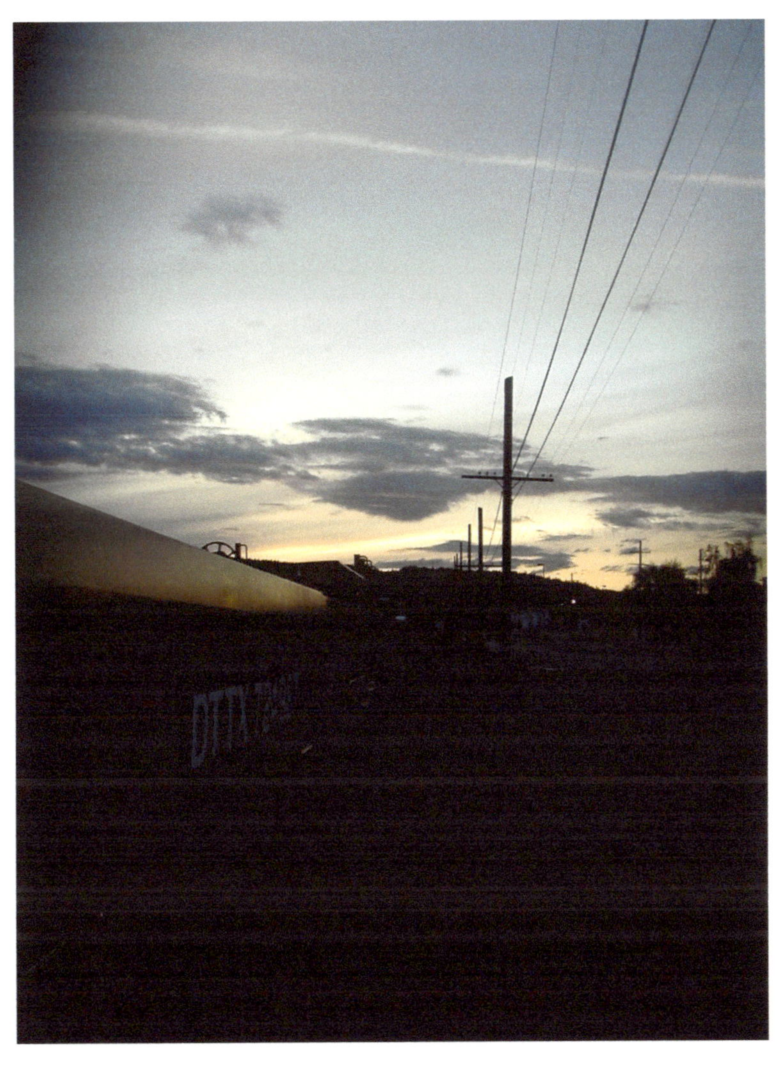

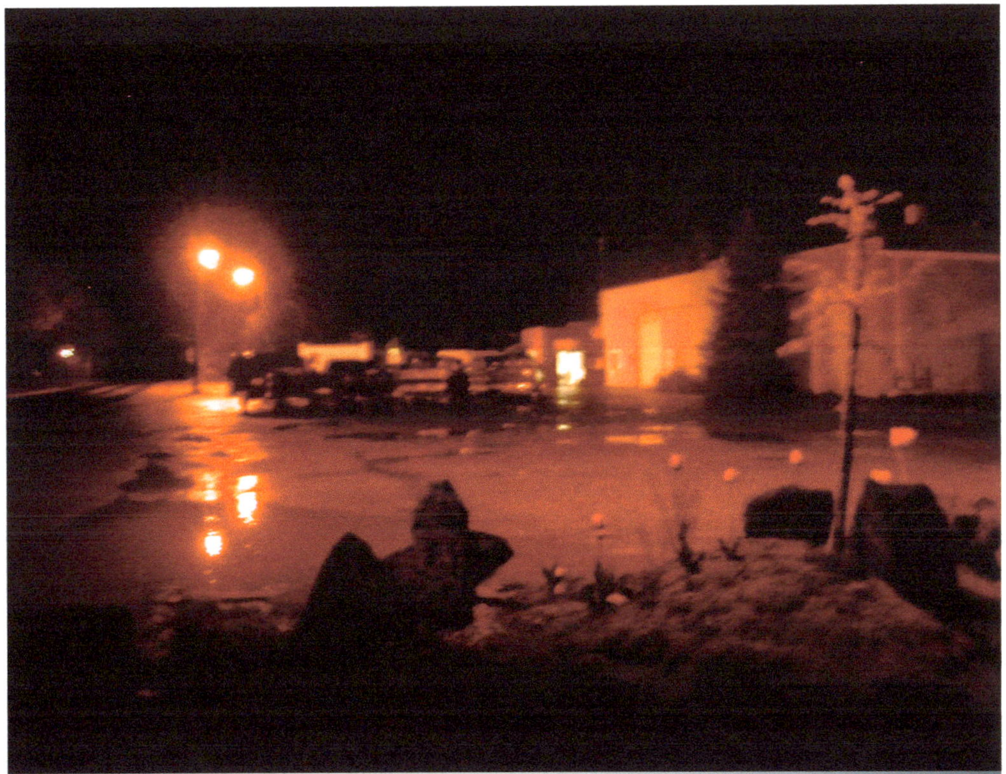

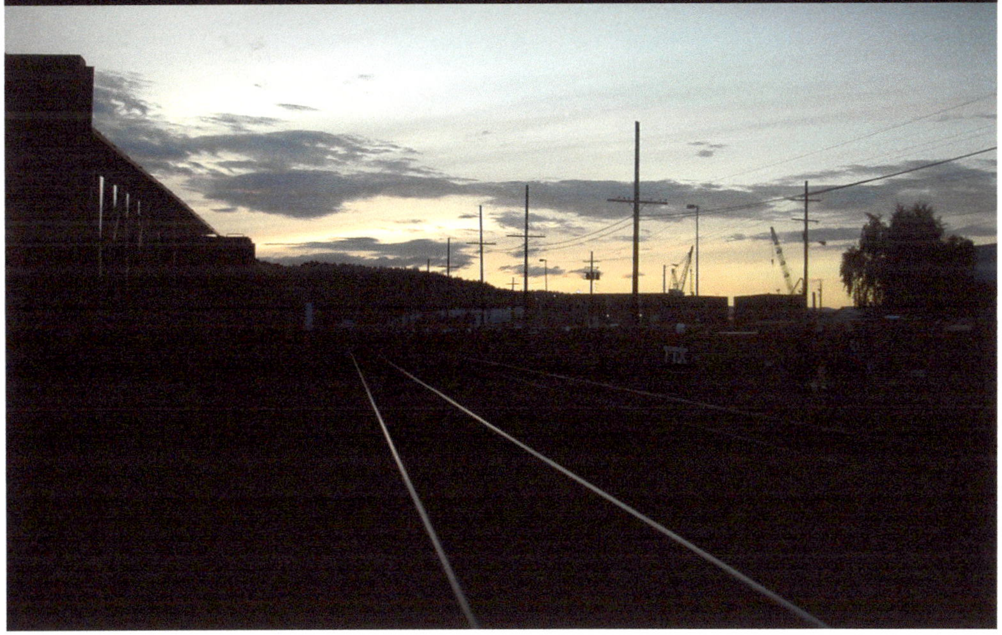

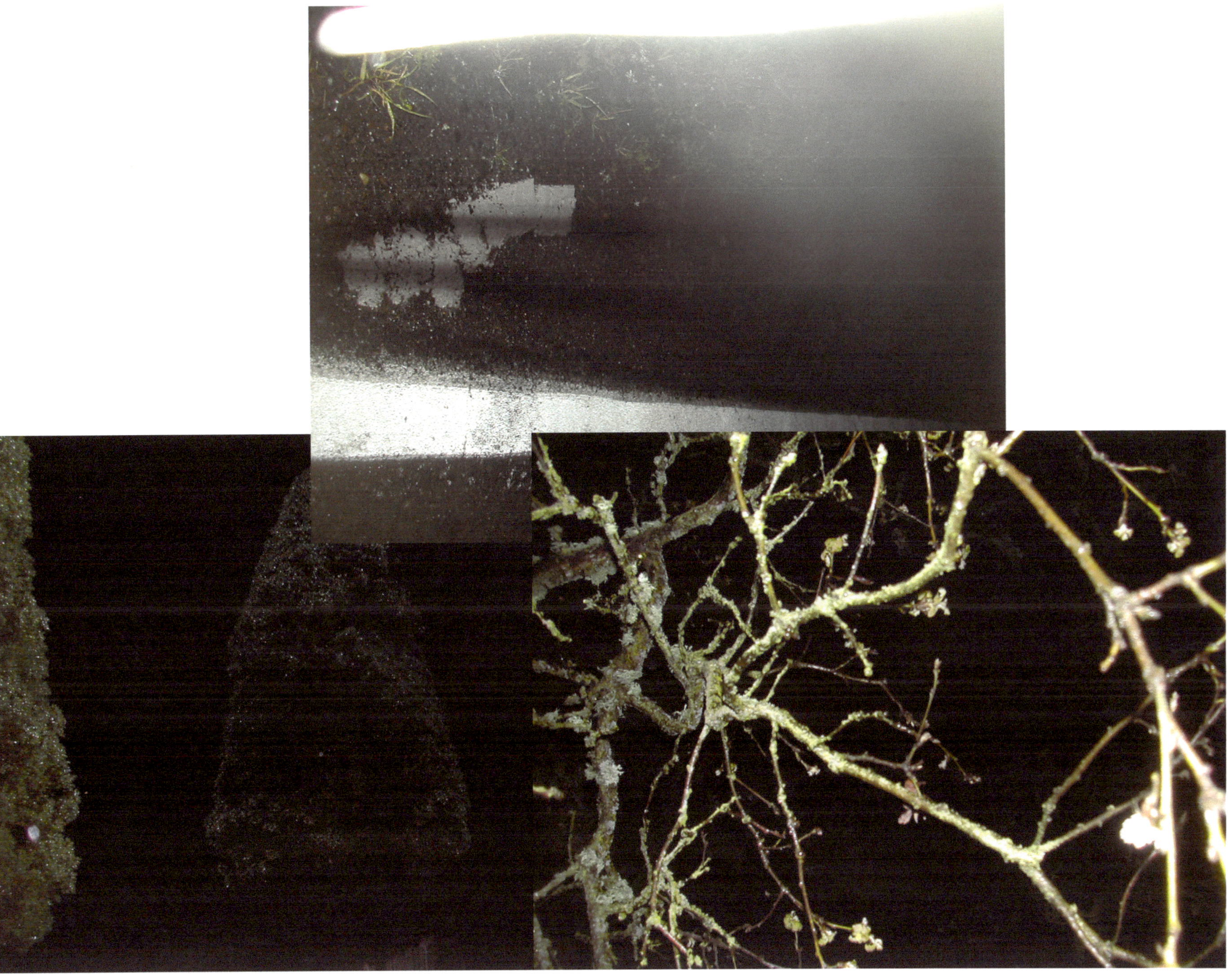

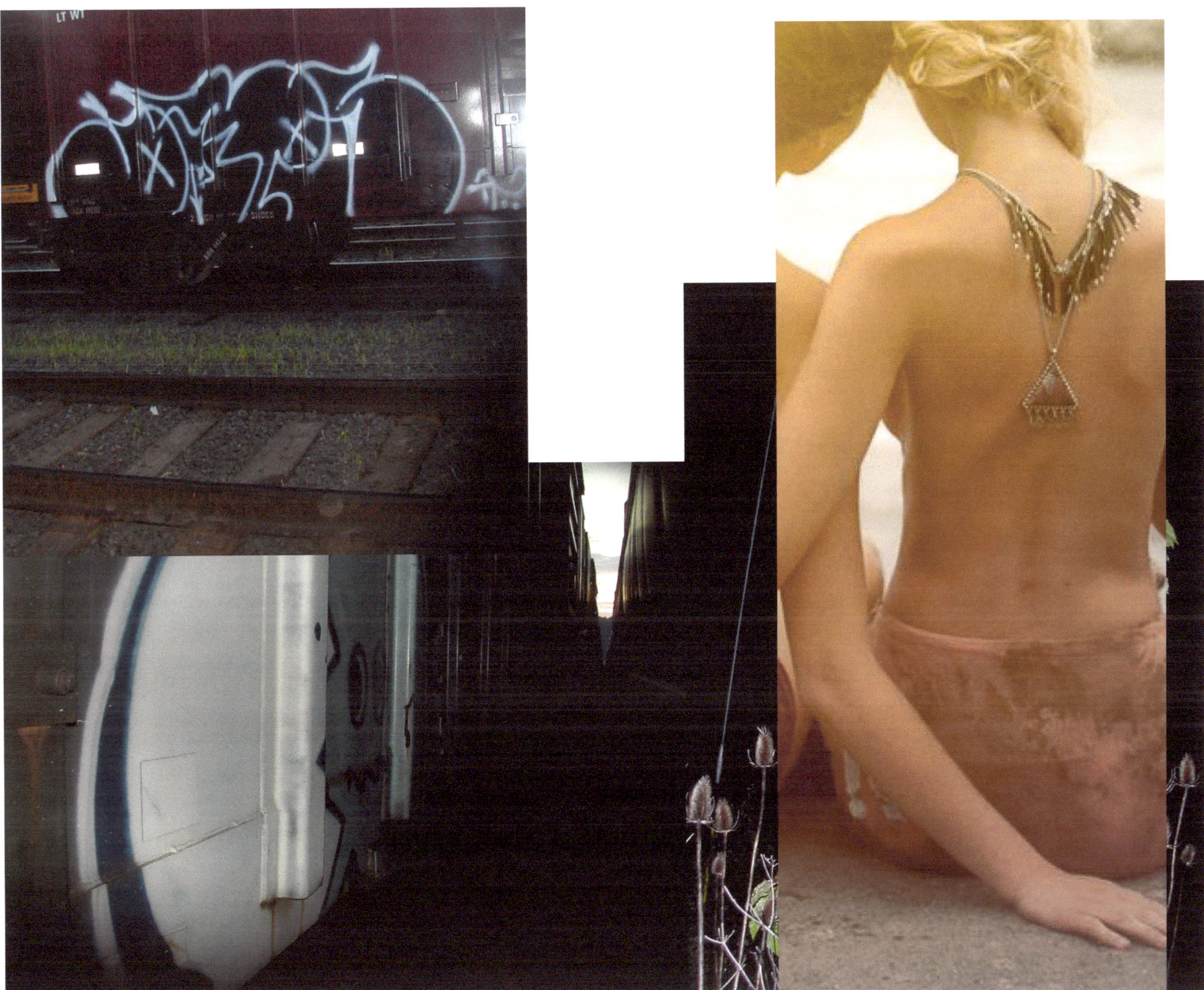

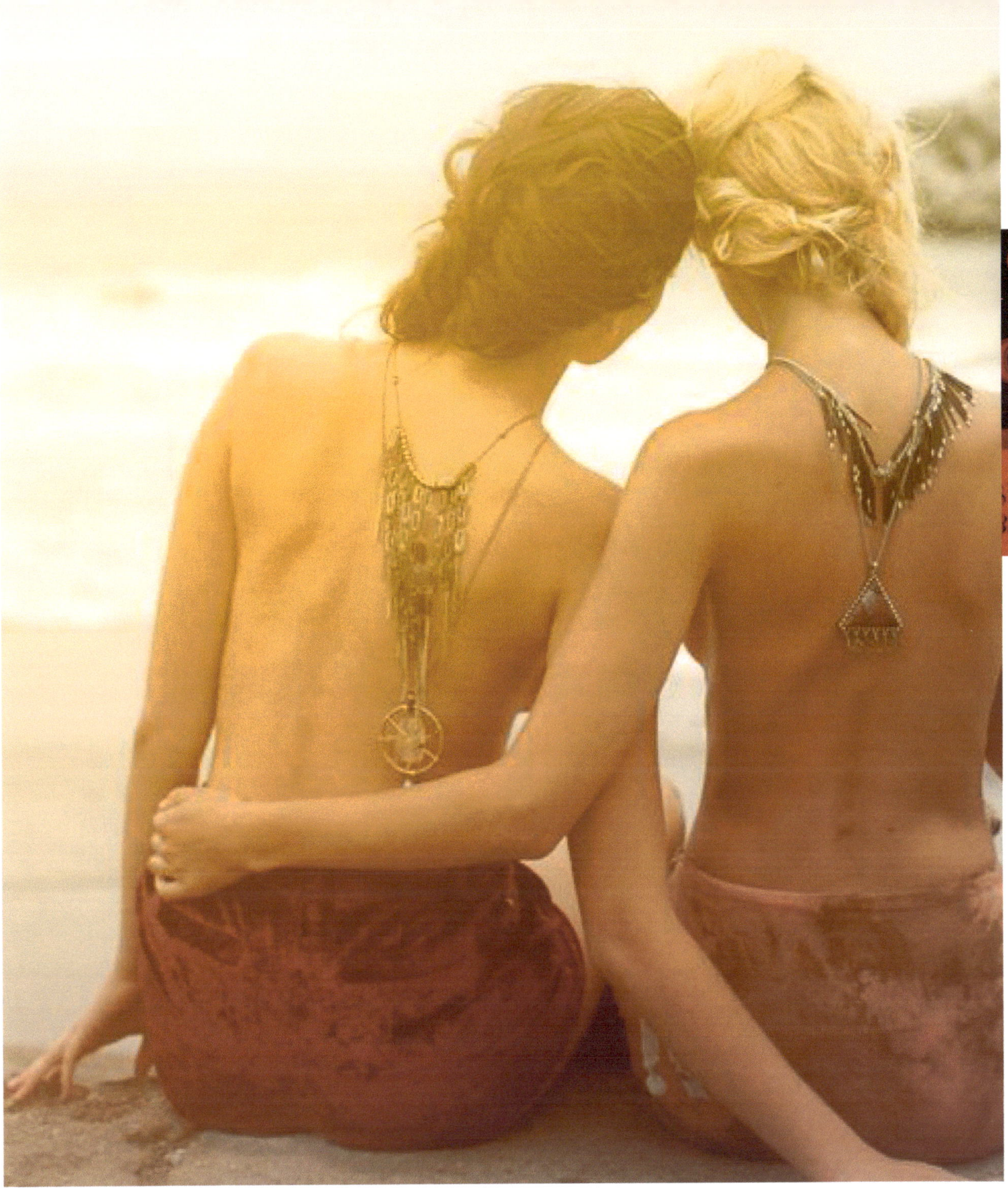

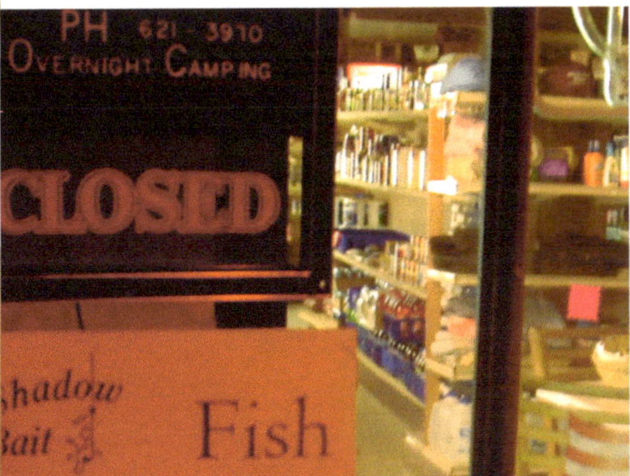

PH 621 - 3970
OVERNIGHT CAMPING
CLOSED
Shadow
Bait
Fish

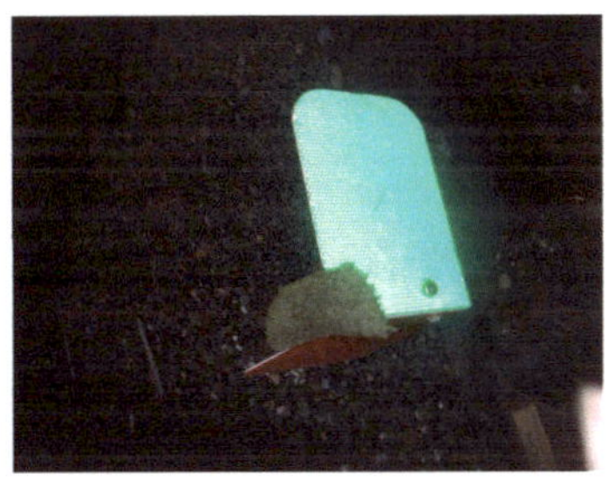

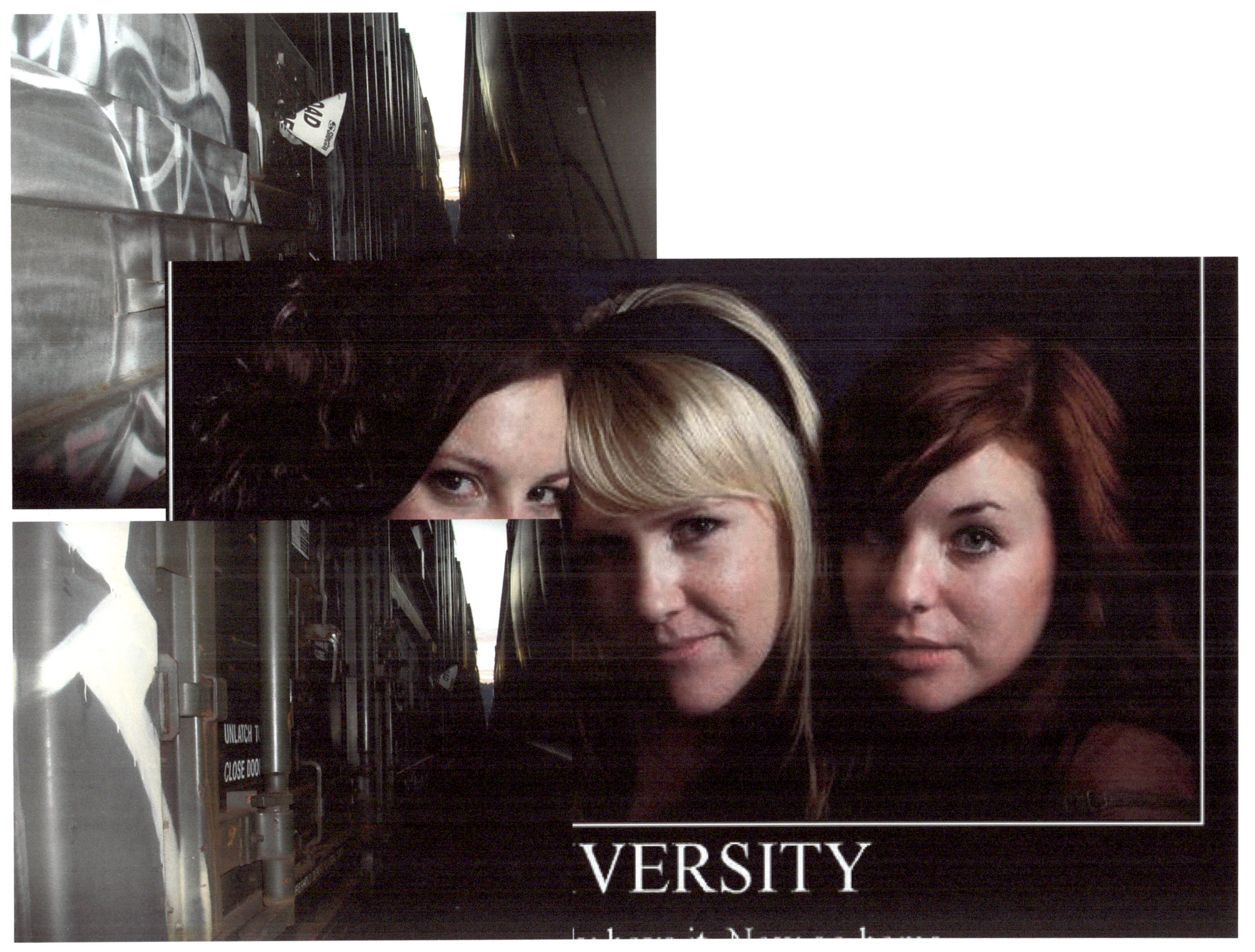
VERSITY

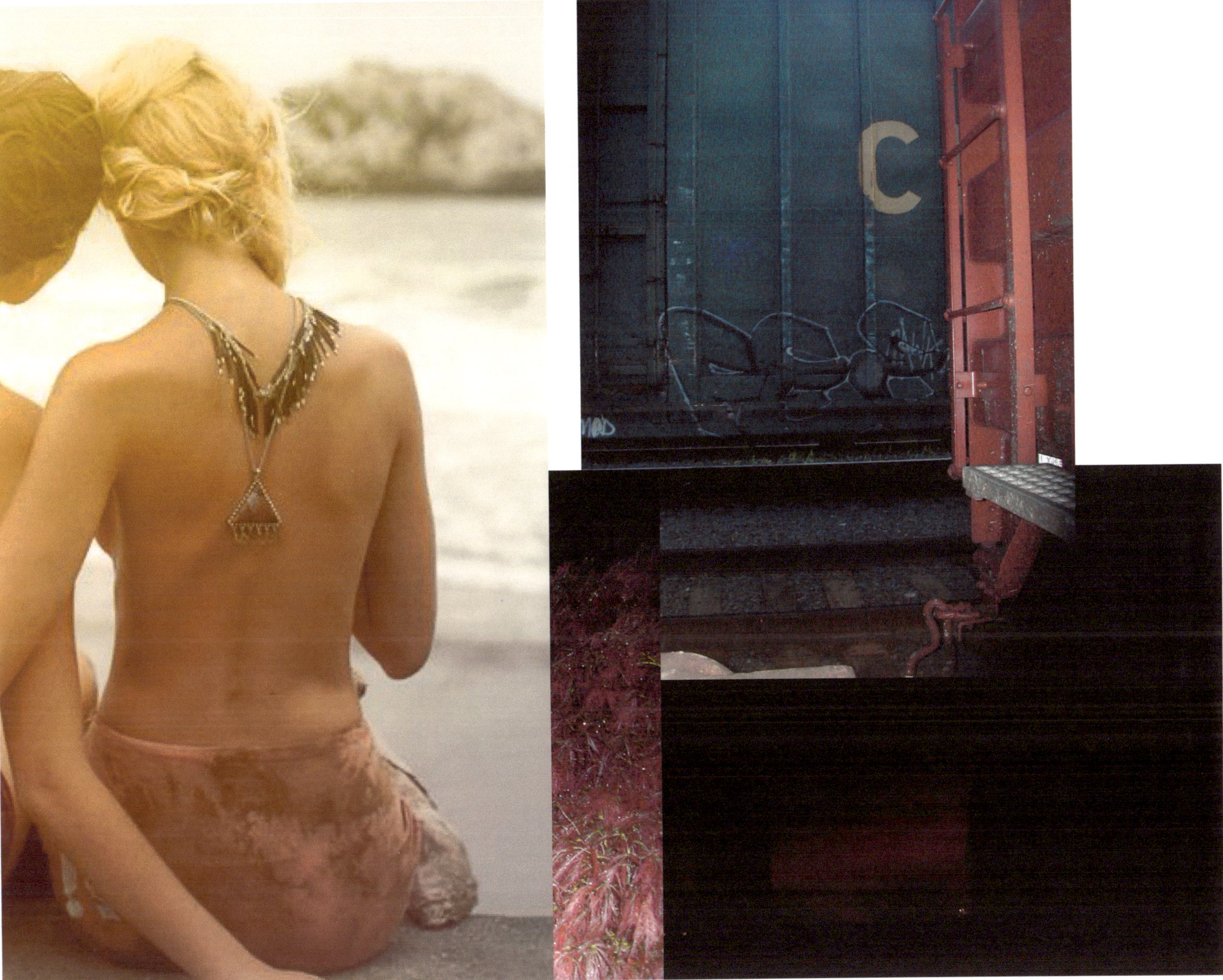

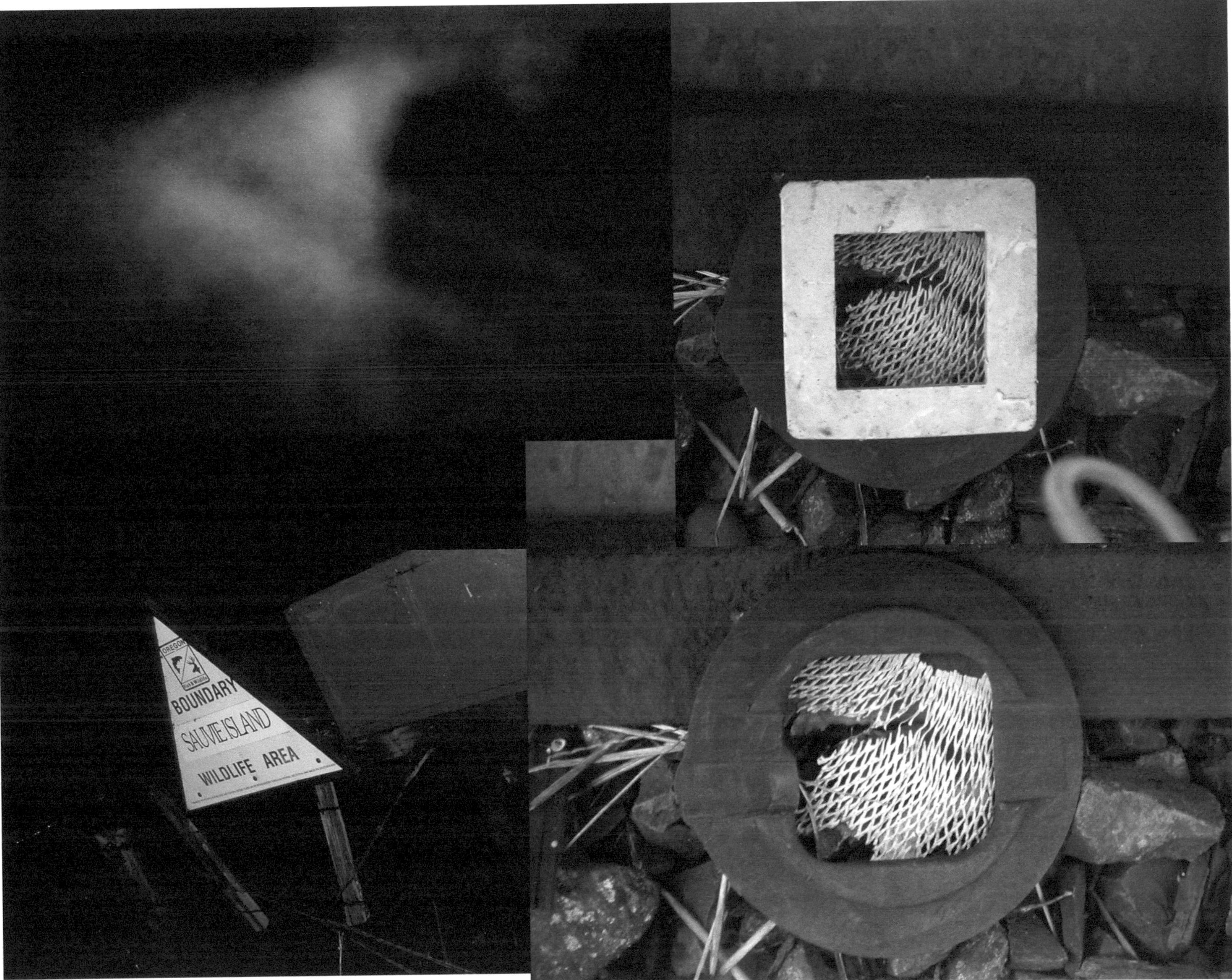
OREGON
BOUNDARY
SAUVIE ISLAND
WILDLIFE AREA

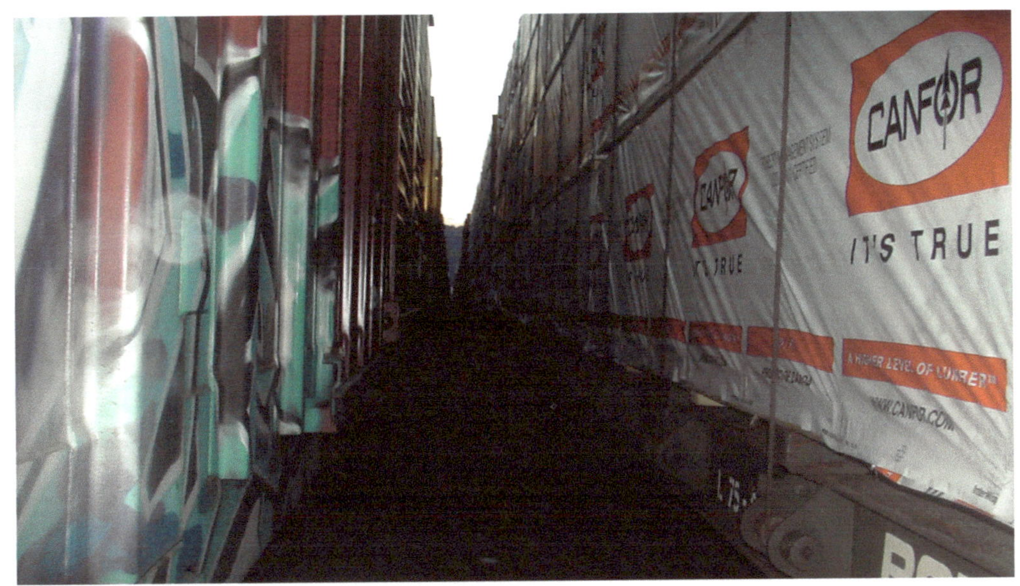

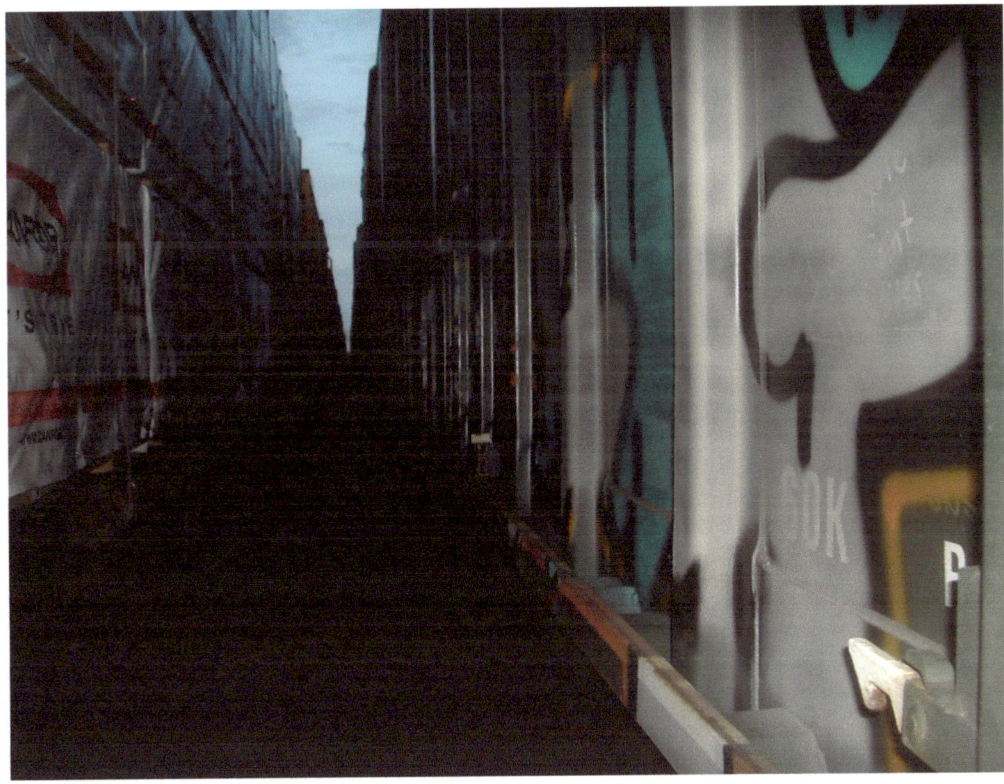

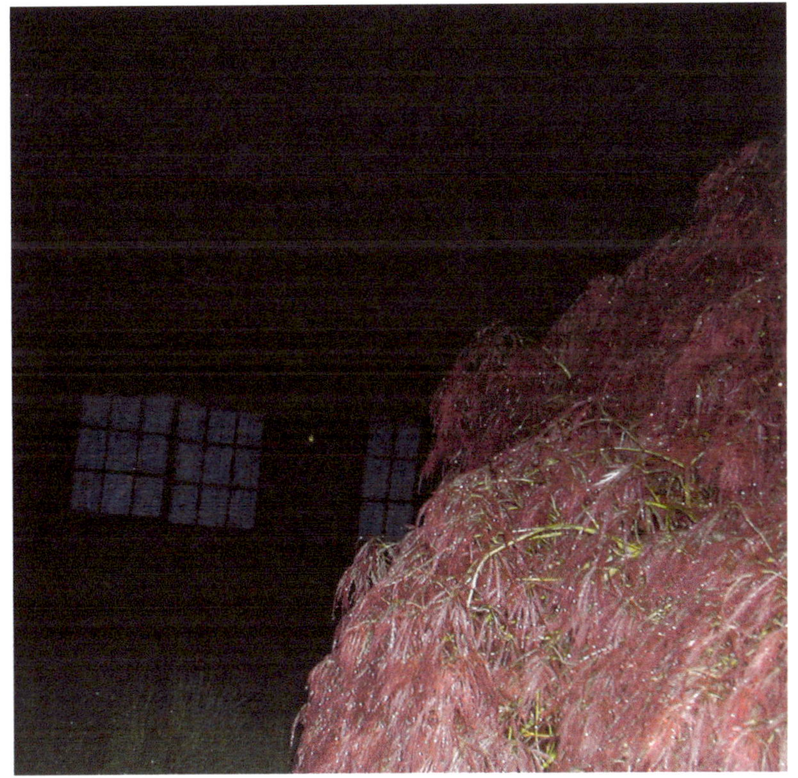

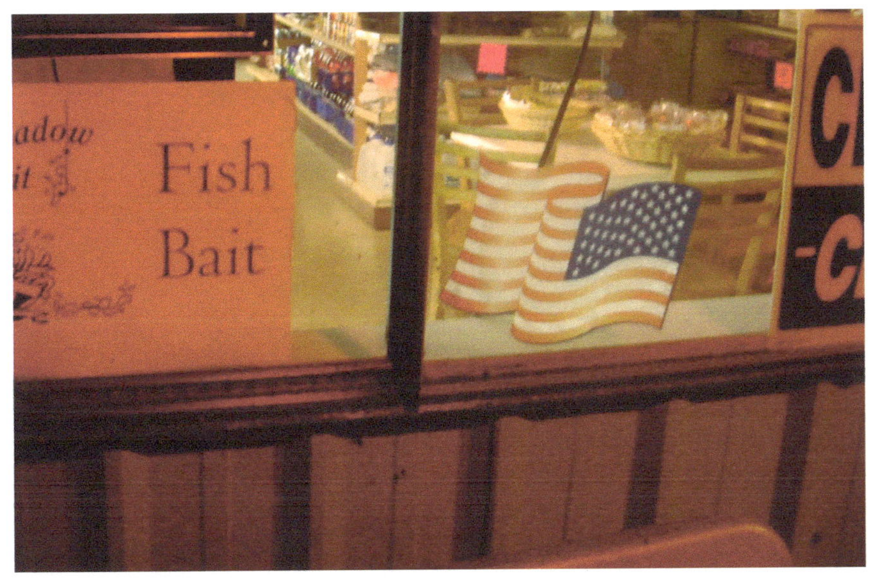

adow
it
Fish
Bait
CI
-CI

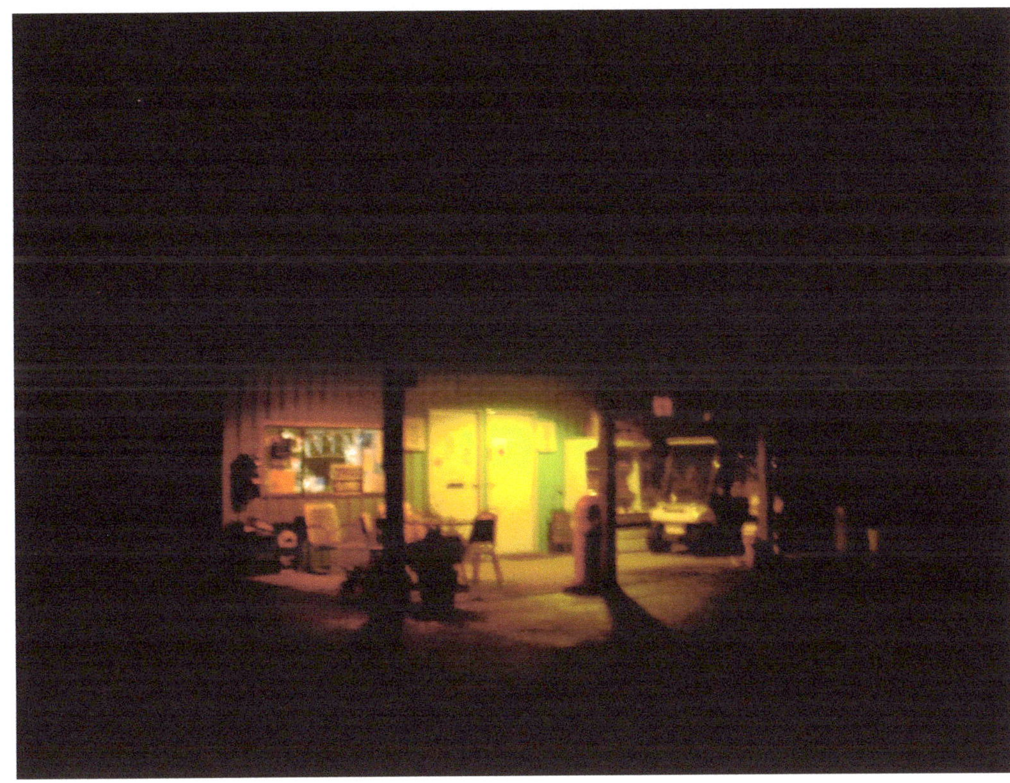

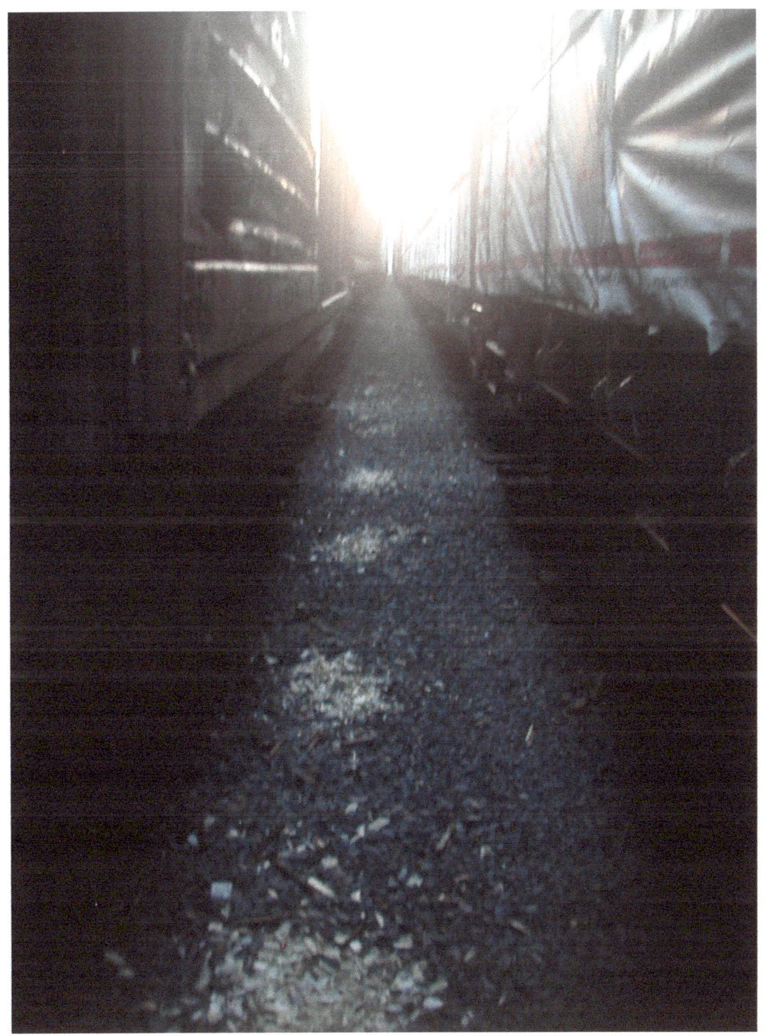

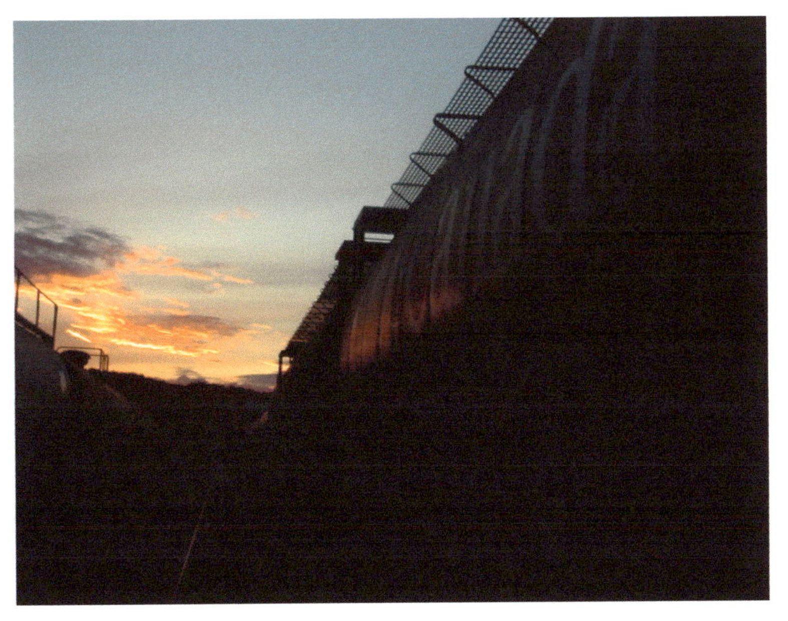
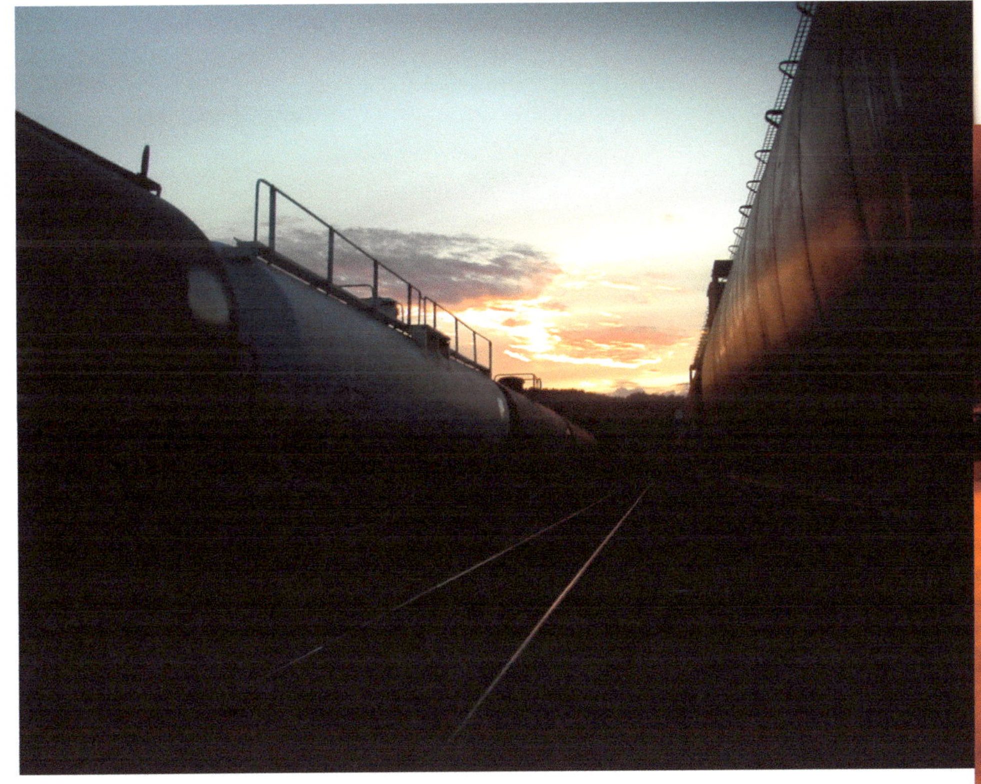

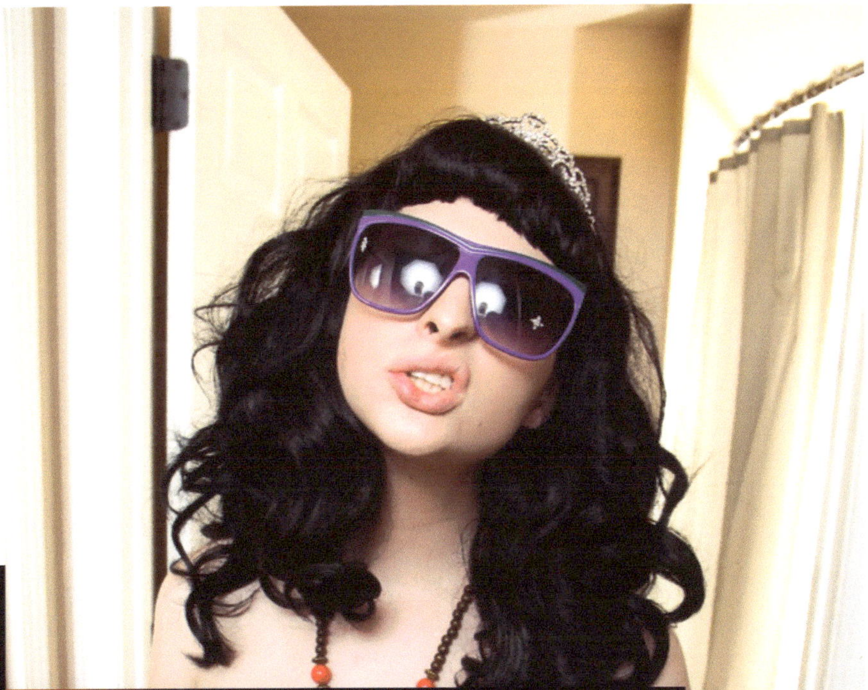

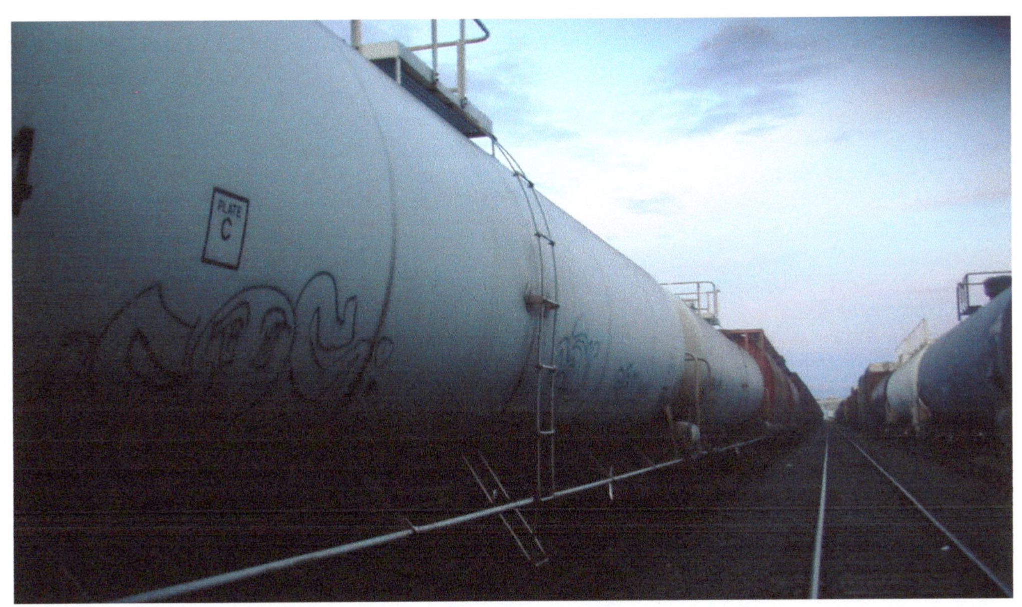

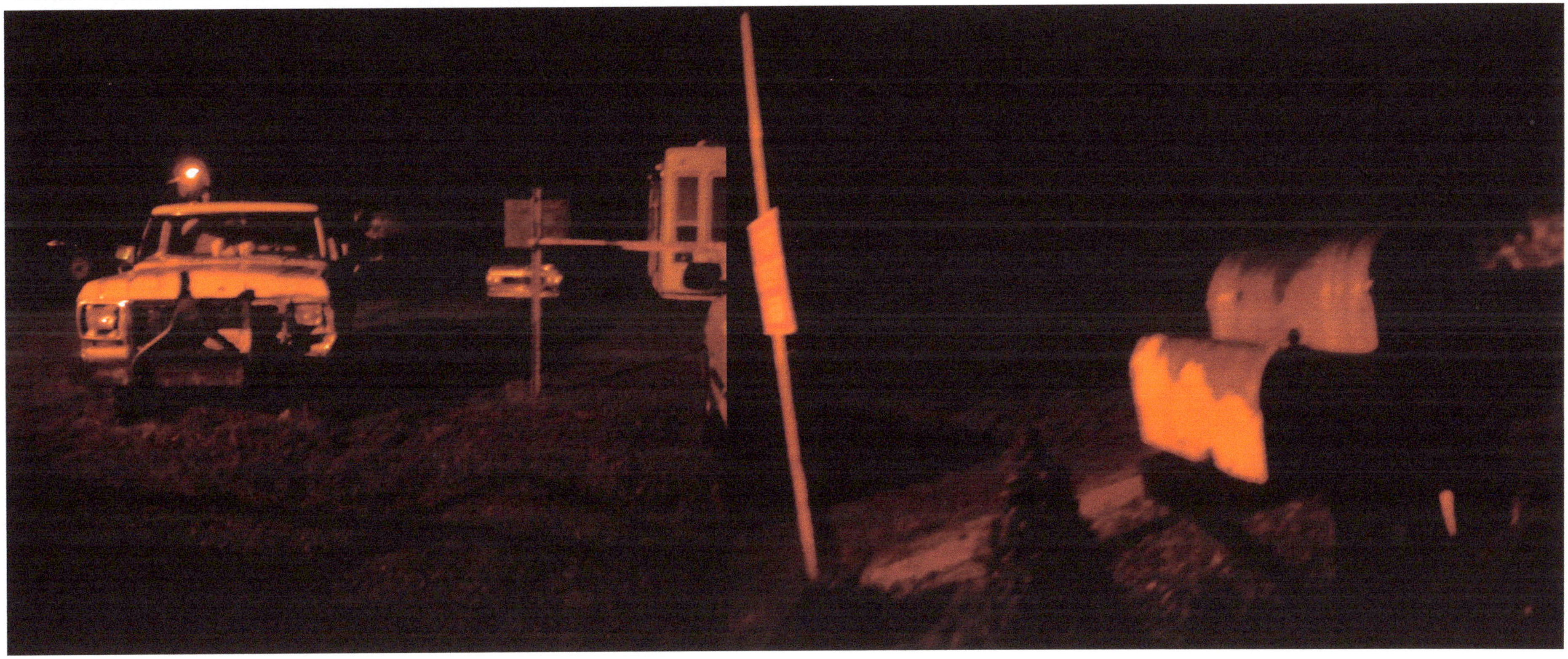

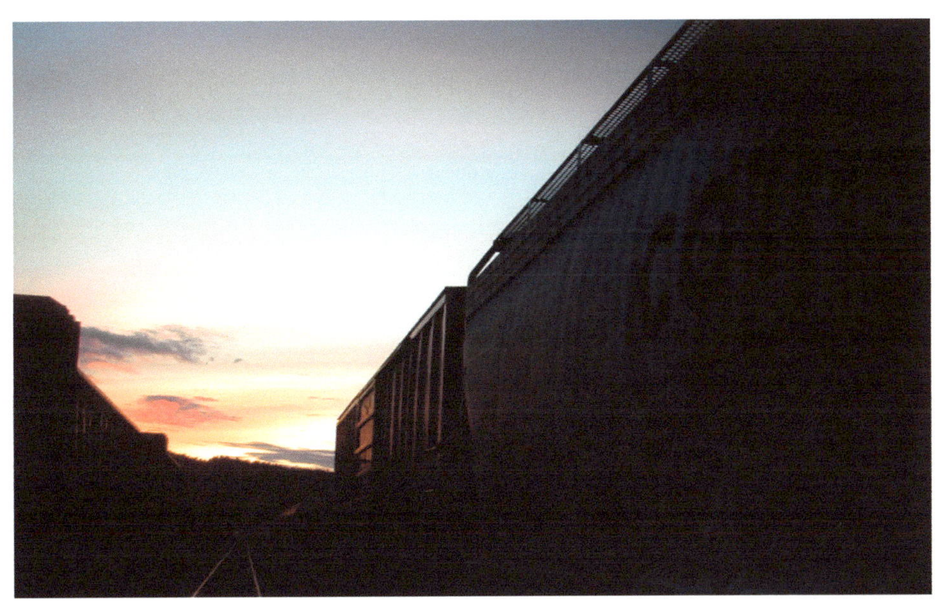

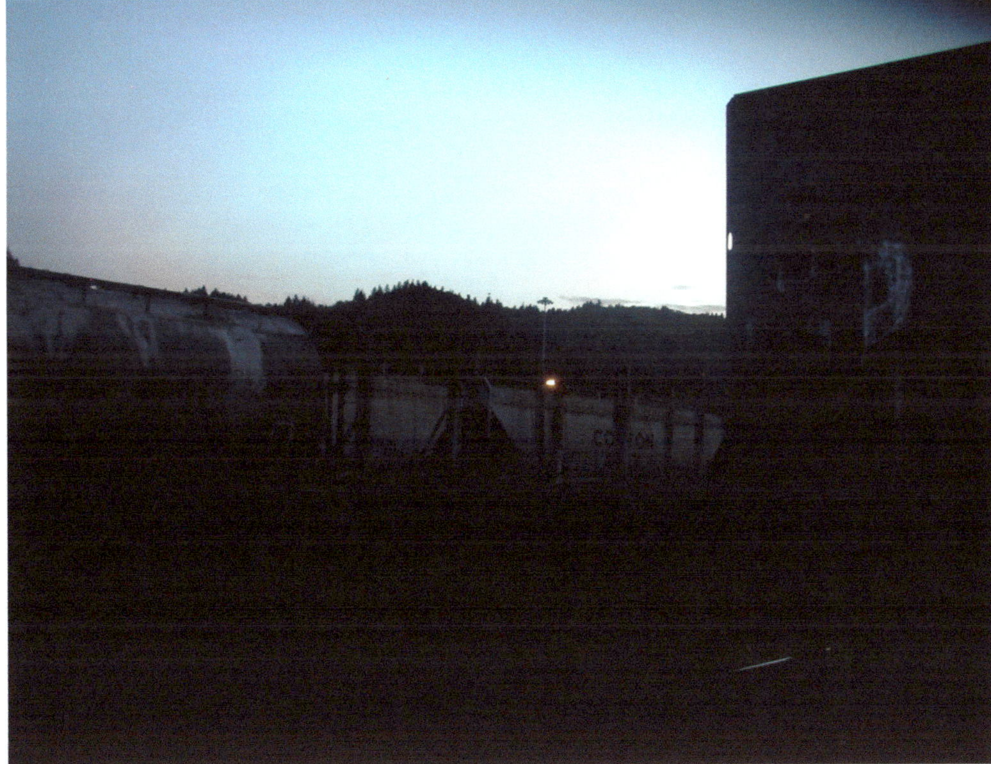

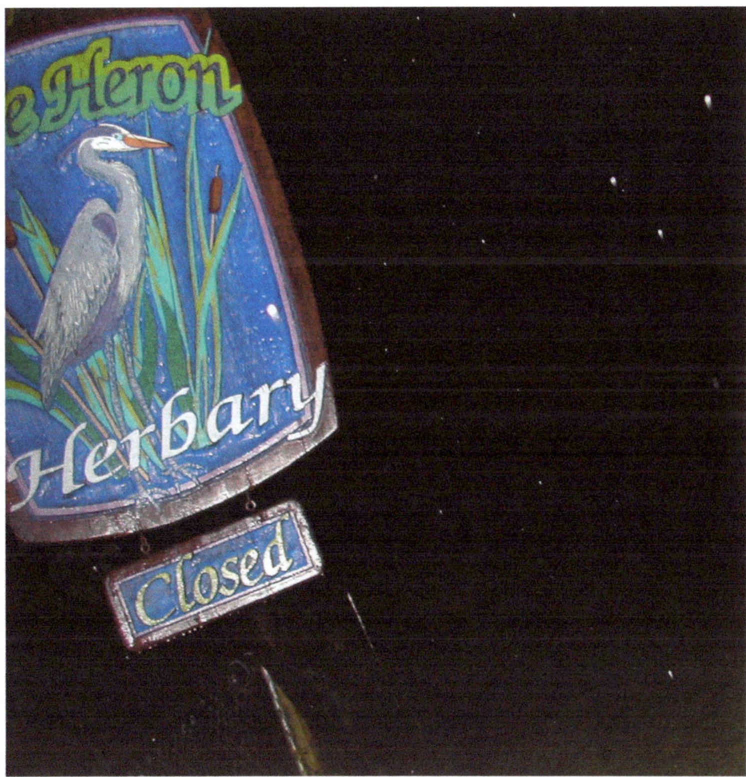
e Heron
Herbary
Closed

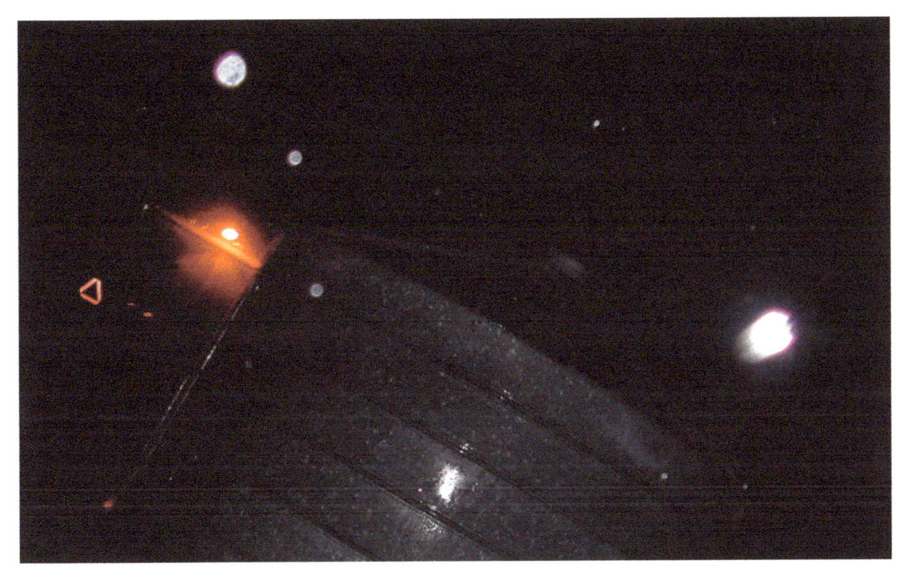

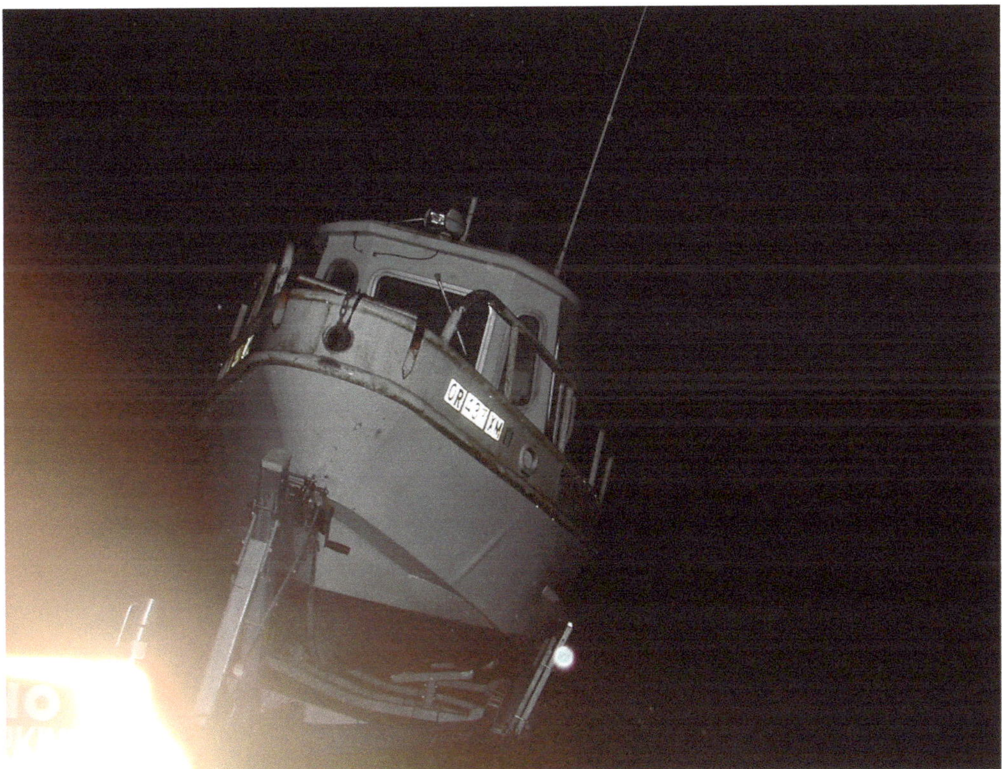

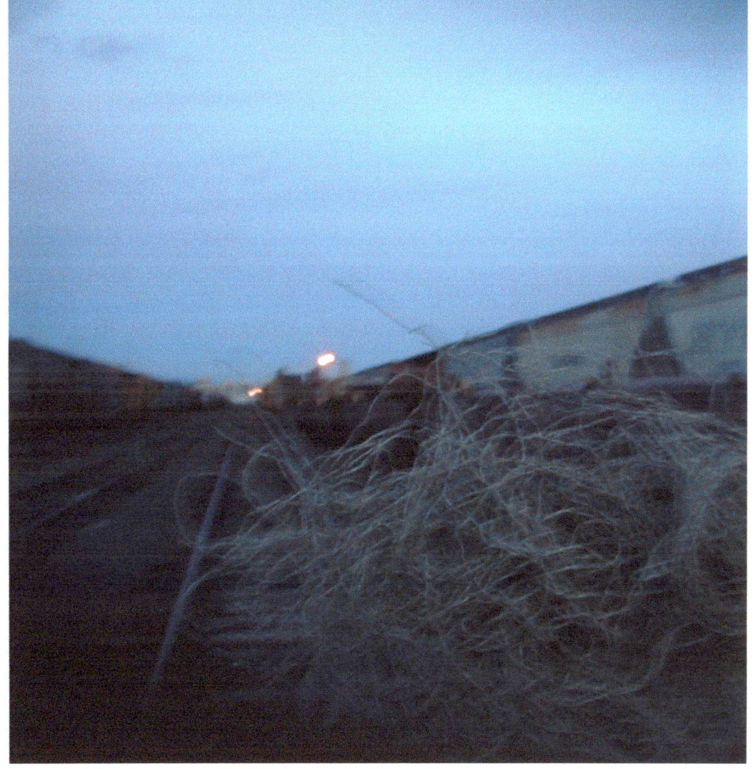

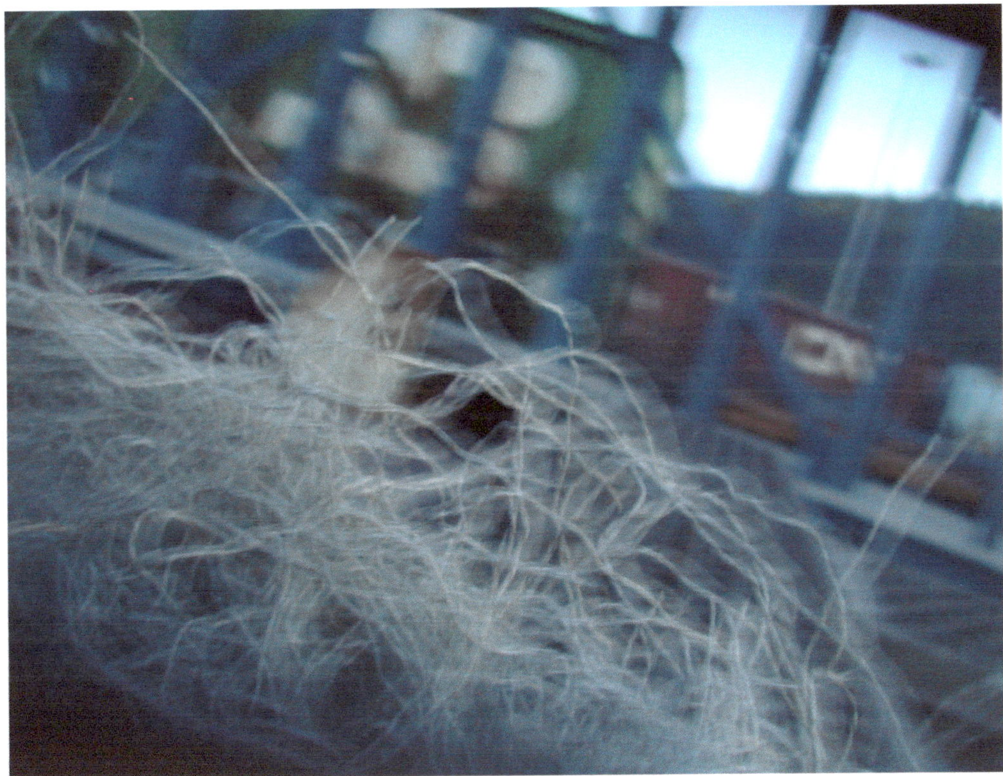

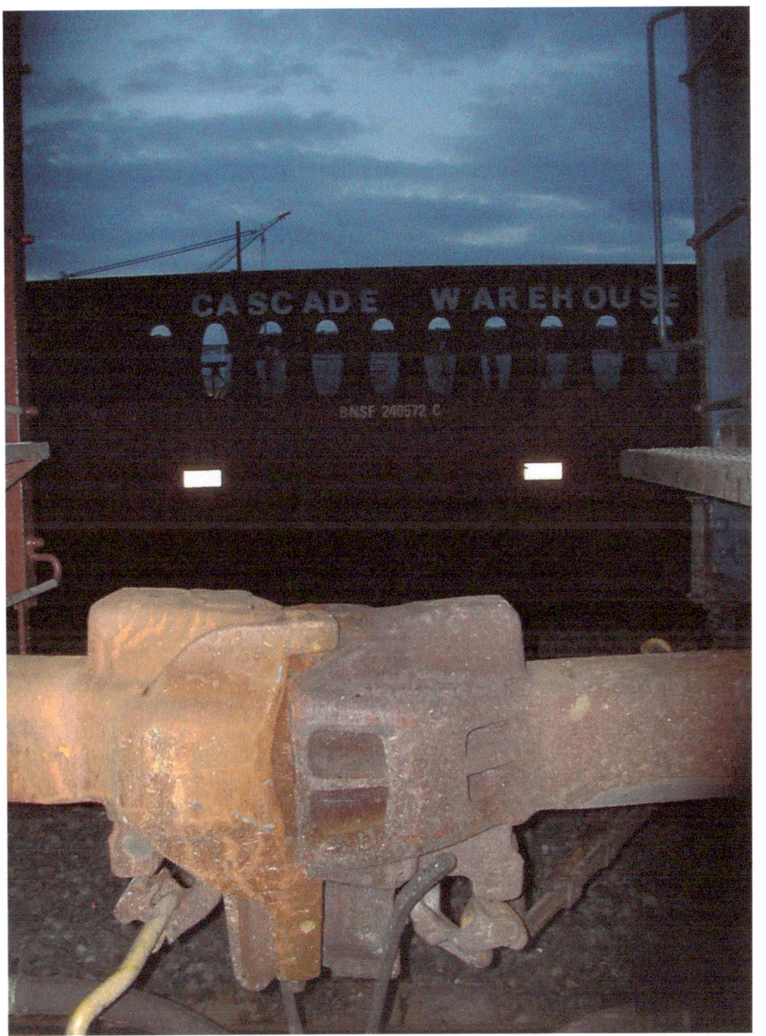
CASCADE   WAREHOUSE
BNSF 240572 C

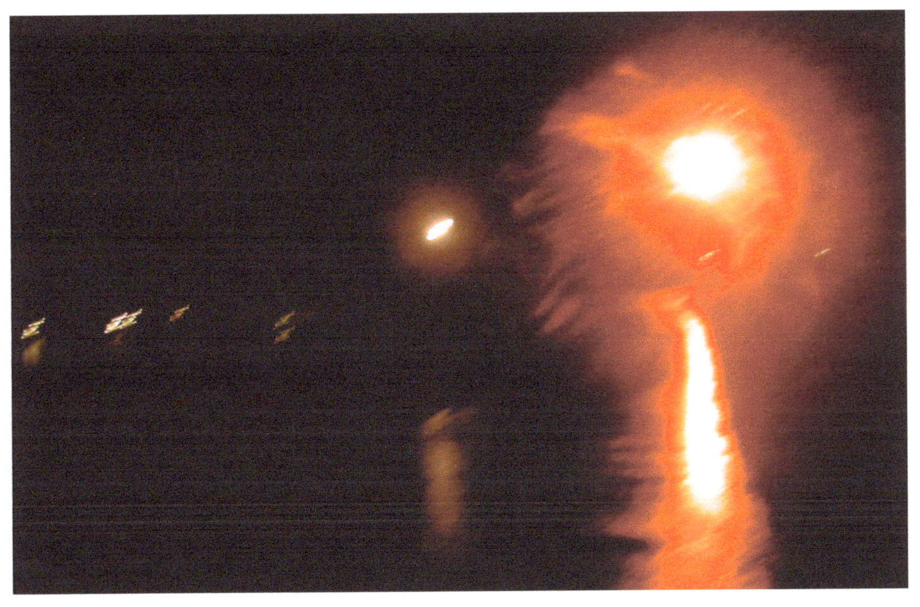
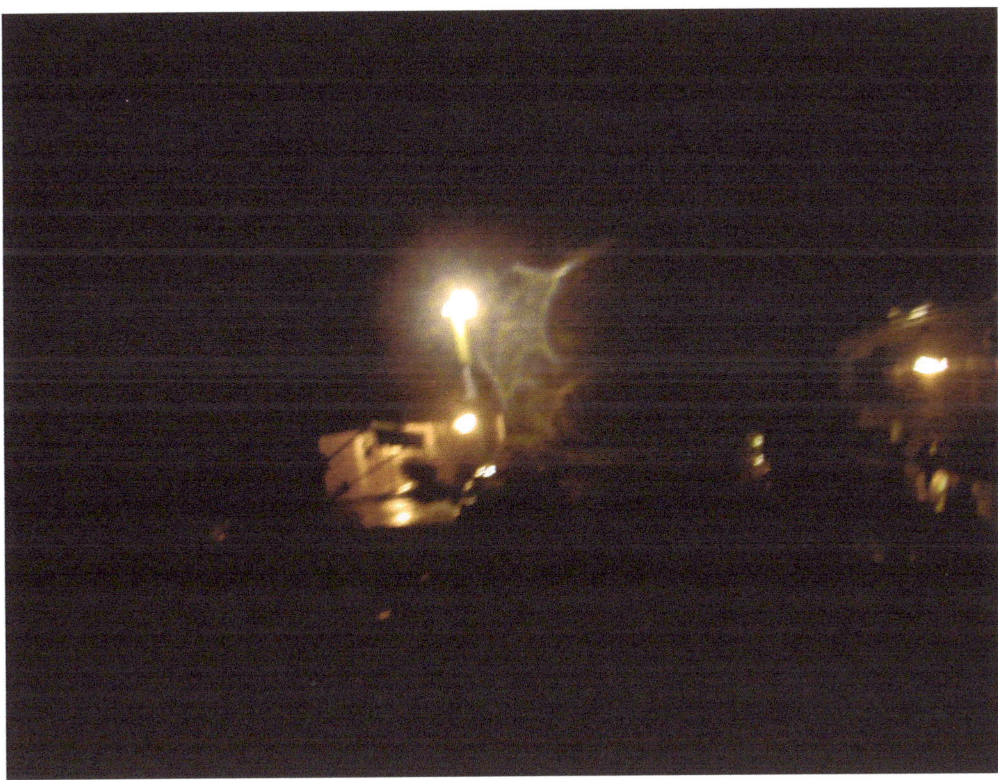
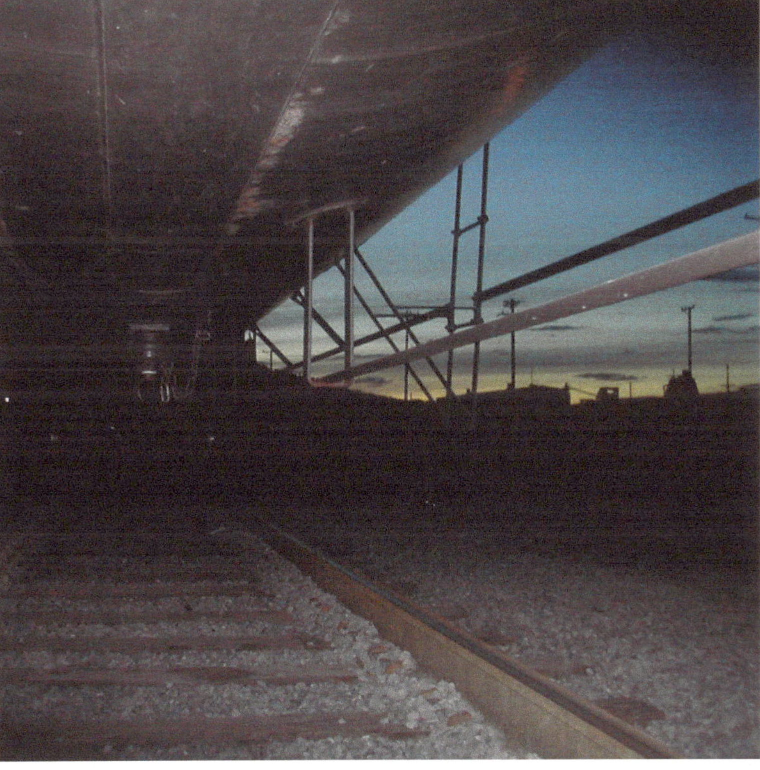

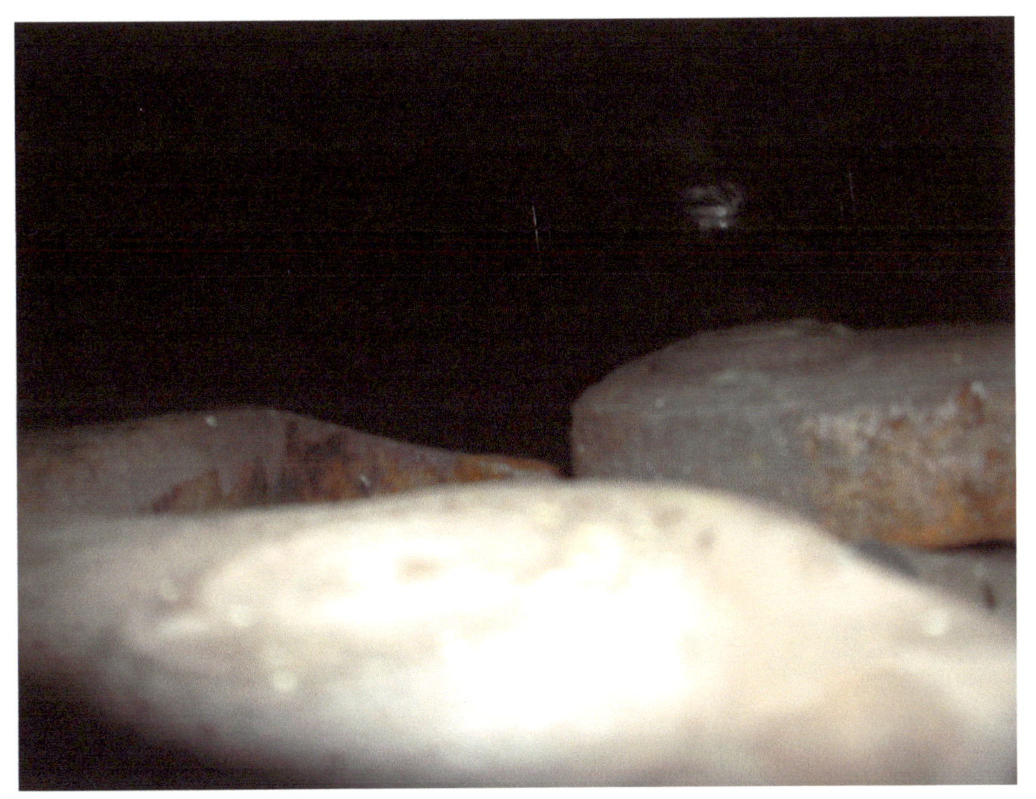

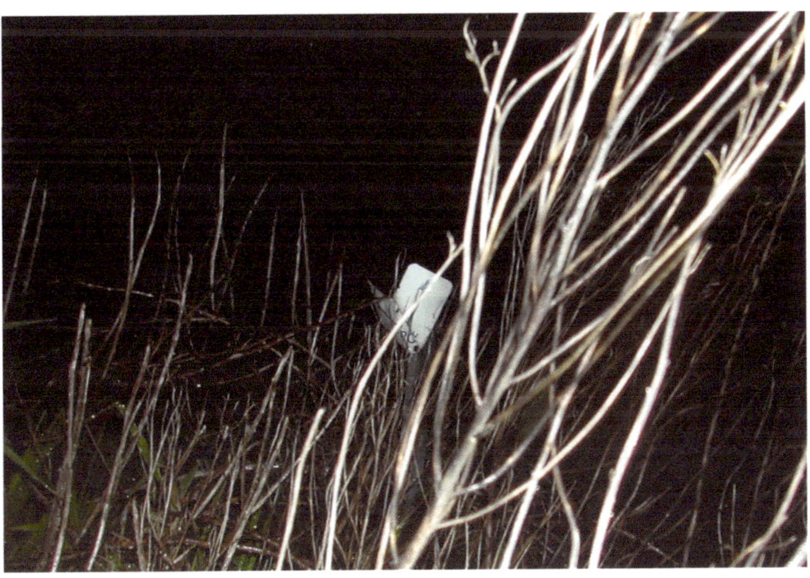

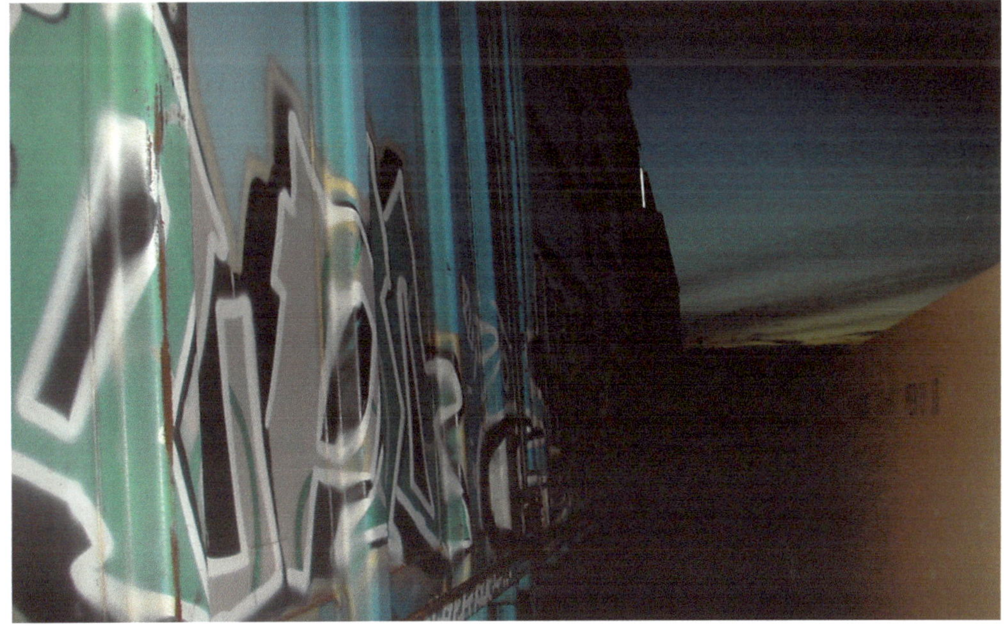

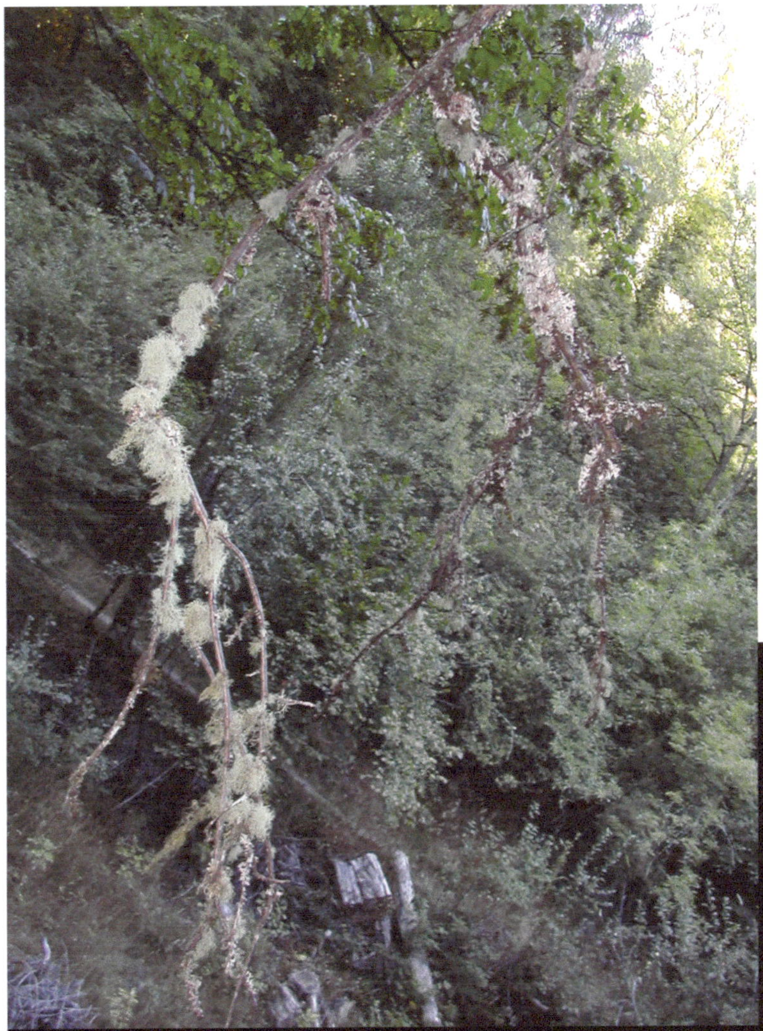

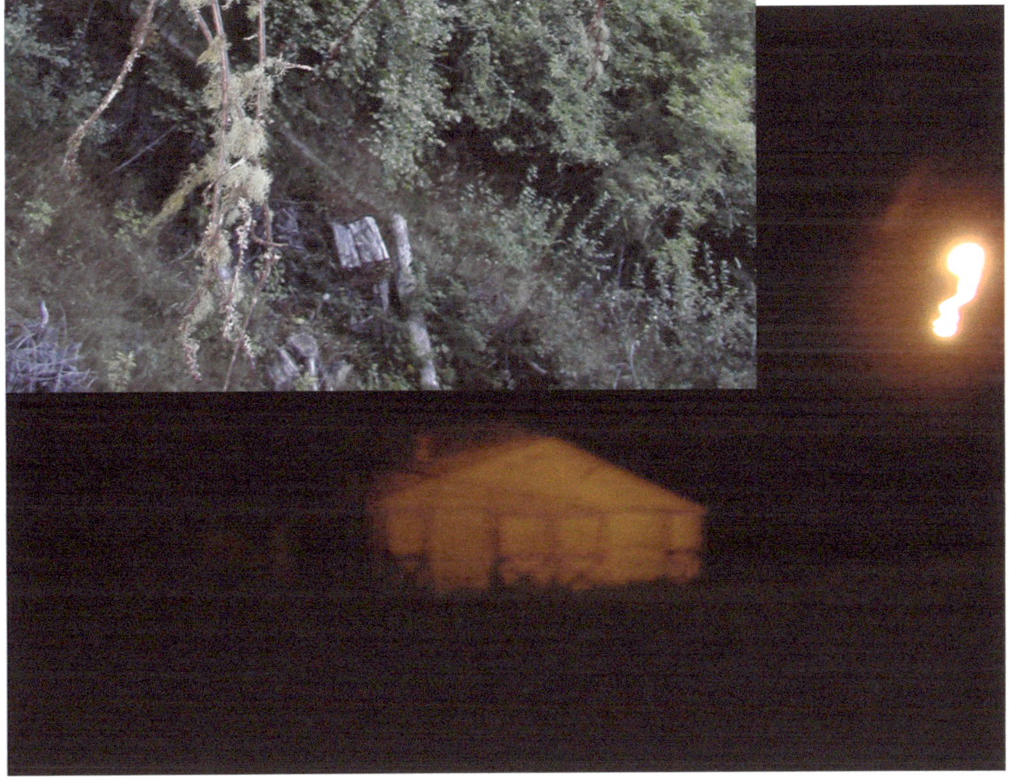

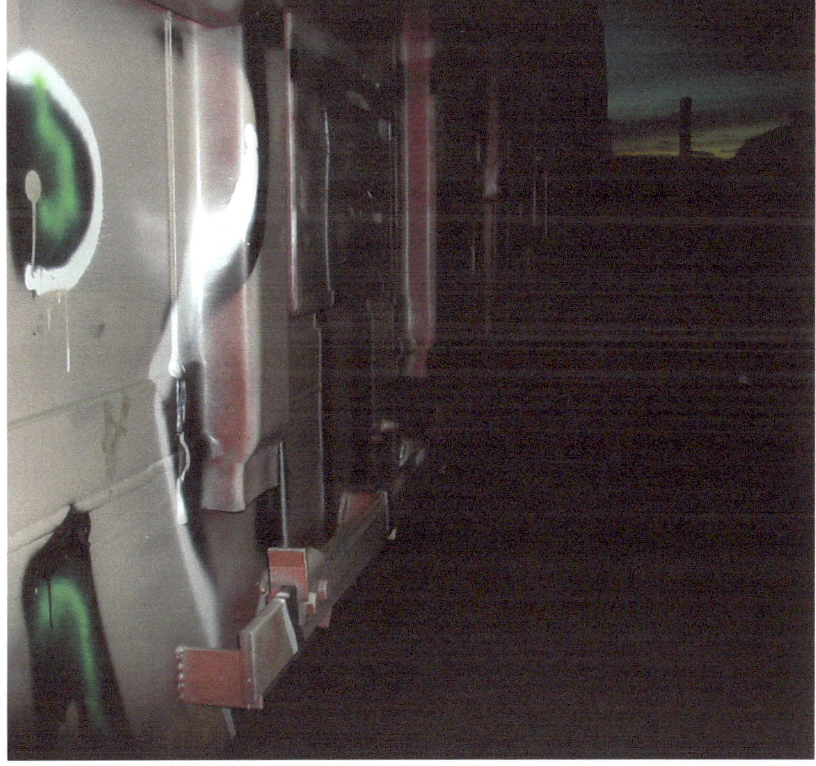

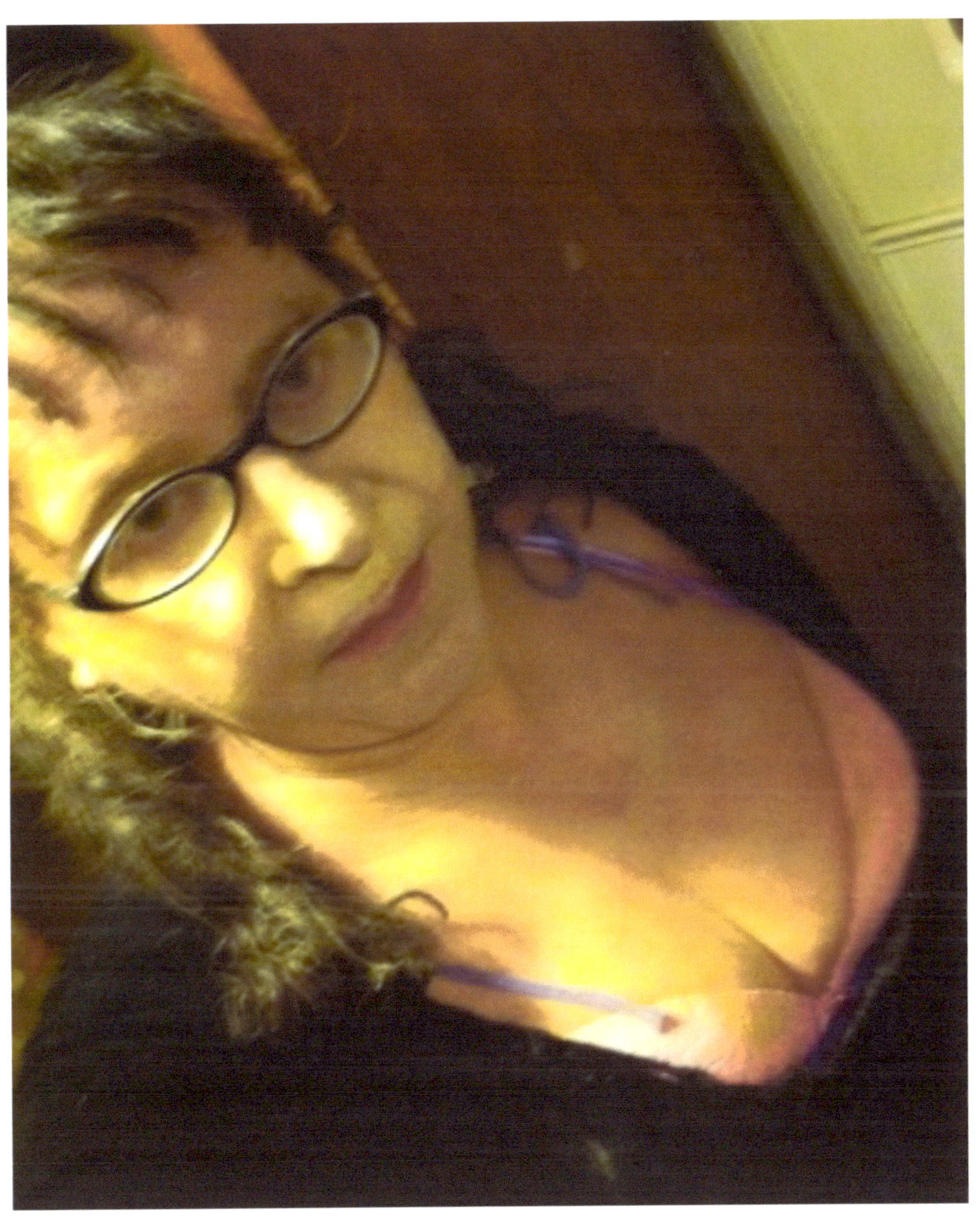

andrea arthena